Ruth Prawer Jhabvala

Twayne's English Authors Series

Kinley E. Roby, Editor

Northeastern University

TEAS 494

RUTH PRAWER JHABVALA
1927—
Photograph by Jerry Bauer

Ruth Prawer Jhabvala

Ralph J. Crane

University of Waikato

Twayne Publishers • New York
Maxwell Macmillan Canada • Toronto
Maxwell Macmillan International • New York   Oxford   Singapore   Sydney

Twayne's English Authors Series No. 494.
Ruth Prawer Jhabvala
Ralph J. Crane

Twayne Publishers   Maxwell Macmillan Canada, Inc.
Macmillan Publishing Company   1200 Eglinton Avenue East
866 Third Avenue   Suite 200
New York, New York 10022   Don Mills, Ontario M3C 3N1

Library of Congress Cataloging-in-PublicationData

Crane, Ralph J., 1957—
    Ruth Prawer Jhabvala / Ralph J. Crane.
        p.   cm.—(Twayne's English authors series : TEAS 494)
    Includes bibliographical references and index.
    ISBN 0-8057-7030-5 (alk. paper)
    1. Jhabvala, Ruth Prawer, 1927–   —Criticism and interpretation.
2. India in literature, I. Title. II. Series.
PR9499.3.J5Z65   1992
823—dc20   92-11257
                                                            CIP

The paper used in this publication meets the minimum requirements
of American National Standard for Information Sciences—Permanence
of Paper for Printed Library Materials. ANSI Z3948-1984.∞™

10 9 8 7 6 5 4 3 2 1

Printed in the United States of America

*For my
mother and father
and for Joy*

Contents

Preface

In 1980 I visited India for the first time. I had read E. M. Forster's *A Passage to India* and J. G. Farrell's *The Siege of Krishnapur* before I went, but, of course, neither prepared me for the India I found. During the two months of that first visit I absorbed a tantalizing hint of India, a melting-pot memory of mingling smells, tastes, sounds, and sights. India has fascinated me ever since. On returning to England I began to read eagerly every novel about India I came across—Anglo-Indian and Indo-Anglian alike—and thus I discovered the fiction of Ruth Prawer Jhabvala. Having been seduced by one India, the India I discovered for myself, I was later seduced by another, the India of Ruth Prawer Jhabvala's fiction. Her work continues to captivate me, though not through any misguided notion that her India is the "real" India (whatever that is), or because her India corresponds to my own (it doesn't). Yet on a recent visit to India I recall waking and looking out of the window of my room in the YMCA hostel in New Delhi and seeing vultures on the roof of a nearby building, silhouetted against a brilliant blue sky of Jhabvalan proportions.

Ruth Prawer Jhabvala has now been publishing for almost 40 years. She has published 10 novels and 5 collections of stories (including a volume of selected stories) and has had 17 screenplays produced. This book restricts itself to a discussion of Jhabvala's fiction; I have not discussed her writing for the cinema, which, with the exceptions of *The Householder* and *Autobiography of a Princess*, has not been published.

In keeping with the guidelines for this series, this book aims to provide the general reader with a clear, palatable introduction to Jhabvala's fiction. I hope, however, that the specialist reader too will find much food for thought in the pages that follow.

The introductory chapter outlines Jhabvala's biography and emphasizes her complex triple heritage—the complexity and importance of which are implicit in the subsequent chapters' discussion of her fiction. Much of the biographical information is gathered from Jhabvala's Neil Gunn Memorial Lecture, "Disinheritance," and I continue to use that piece and "Myself in India"—the frank essay that introduces her third collection of stories, *An Experience of India*—as gateways to her fiction.

In later chapters I treat the novels chronologically, in groups of two or more works that appear to be linked in terms of theme and subject and in relation to Jhabvala's changing attitude toward India. After examining the Indian novels I devote a chapter to the short stories, many of which share much in common with the novels discussed, while others look ahead to the subjects of the two most recent novels. This arrangement is also in keeping with the chronological structure of this book, for all the stories were published before *In Search of Love and Beauty* and *Three Continents*.

Without overstressing the importance of the literary influences that have been at work on Jhabvala, I have considered the influence of E. M. Forster's *A Passage to India* in some depth in relation to three of her novels—*A Backward Place, A New Dominion,* and *Heat and Dust*—because I believe these works reflect a deliberate response to a novel that holds a monumental position in the Anglo-Indian canon, and casts a large shadow over the Indo-Anglian canon as well. Jhabvala's response to *A Passage to India* might well be a case of what Salman Rushdie calls the empire writing back to the center.

Acknowledgments

I would like to thank two people who have provided me with invaluable advice and encouragement. First is Dr Jennifer Livett, who read the manuscript and whose perceptive, detailed comments enabled me to improve my text considerably. The shortcomings that remain are, as they say, my own. Second is my wife, Joy, who has supported me in many ways and who has again shared the burden of proofreading. I would also like to thank the University of Otago, New Zealand, for financial assistance in the form of a postdoctoral research fellowship from July 1990 to January 1992.

I am grateful to John Murray (Publishers) Ltd. for allowing me to quote from the following works by Ruth Prawer Jhabvala: *Esmond in India, The Householder, Get Ready for Battle, Like Birds, like Fishes, A Backward Place, A Stronger Climate, An Experience of India, A New Dominion, Heat and Dust, How I Became a Holy Mother, In Search of Love and Beauty,* and *Three Continents.* Penguin Books Ltd. has granted me permission to quote from *To Whom She Will* and *The Nature of Passion.*

Chronology

1927 Ruth Prawer born in Cologne, Germany.

1939 Family flees from Nazi Germany and settles in England.

1948 Becomes naturalized British citizen.

1951 M.A. in English literature, Queen Mary College, London. Unpublished thesis, "The Short Story in England, 1700–1750." Marries Cyrus S. H. Jhabvala and moves to India.

1955 *To Whom She Will* (novel); published in the United States as *Amrita* (1956).

1956 *The Nature of Passion* (novel).

1957 Begins publishing stories in the *New Yorker*.

1958 *Esmond in India* (novel).

1960 *The Householder* (novel).

1961 Begins association with filmmakers James Ivory and Ishmail Merchant.

1962 *Get Ready for Battle* (novel).

1963 *Like Birds, like Fishes* (short stories). *The Householder* (film).

1965 *A Backward Place* (novel). *Shakespeare Wallah* (film).

1968 *A Stronger Climate* (short stories).

1969 *The Guru* (film).

1970 *Bombay Talkie* (film).

1971 *An Experience of India* (short stories).

1972 *A New Dominion* (novel); published in the United States as *Travelers* (1973).

1973 *Autobiography of a Princess* (film).

1975 *Heat and Dust* (novel). *The Place of Peace* (television film). Is awarded the Booker Prize for fiction. Leaves India and settles in New York.

1976 *How I Became a Holy Mother* (short stories). Receives John Simon Guggenheim Memorial Fellowship.

Chapter One
Amid the Alien Corn
Biography

In an interview published in 1977 Ruth Prawer Jhabvala is quoted as saying, "I don't think there are all that many people who have had just such a varied life as I."[1] By "varied" Jhabvala means geographically and culturally varied. And while Jhabvala may be forgetting how many people were, like herself, expatriated by World War II, the fact remains that she is a writer whose life has been geographically and culturally unsettled, and this unsettlement is reflected in complex ways in her fiction. Her position as a novelist who writes about India is unique. On the one hand, she belongs in the company of such Anglo-Indian writers as Rudyard Kipling, E. M. Forster, and Paul Scott, while on the other, she is equally well placed among such Indo-Anglian writers as R. K. Narayan, Anita Desai, and Kamala Markandaya. She is at once an outsider, a non-Indian, who is also an intimate insider, part of an Indian family. This apparent dichotomy is only one aspect of a cuckoolike life of expatriation that has taken Jhabvala from Europe to India and, most recently, to the United States. This last move, which so far has resulted in two novels set predominantly in America, adds further confusion to the at-best-murky description of Jhabvala as an Indian novelist. Like Joseph Conrad, she resists being defined by her country of birth: "Being a displaced person . . . I've often felt I'm in between, not quite one thing or another."[2] From an early age Ruth Prawer Jhabvala has been destined to be an observer of other cultures—British, Indian, and now American.

Germany

Ruth Prawer Jhabvala was born in Cologne, Germany, on 7 May 1927, the second child of Marcus Prawer, a Polish-Jewish lawyer, and Eleonara Cohn. She has one brother, Siegbert Salomon Prawer, two years her elder.[3] Despite her German birth, Jhabvala's roots do not reach very far into German soil. Her father had come to Germany to escape military conscription in Poland during World War I. There he met her mother, who like Ruth had been born in Cologne, but whose father had come from Russia.

Ruth Prawer Jhabvala's family background was a comfortable, middle-European-bourgeois one of the type she conveys with such brilliant economy in *In Search of Love and Beauty*. The young Ruth Prawer's early childhood memories, when she speaks of them, are of "a well-integrated, solid, assimilated, German-Jewish family" ("Disinheritance," 5), a family whose members proudly identified with the Germany around them. Indeed, one of her mother's proudest moments was being chosen by her school to recite a poem in celebration of the kaiser's birthday, and Ruth Prawer's family treasured the picture of the Cologne Rathaus presented to her grandfather in recognition of his civic virtues. On the other hand, though, the Prawers identified with their Jewishness; Ruth Prawer's maternal grandfather, a respected German gentleman and citizen of Cologne, was also the cantor in Cologne's largest synagogue.

While Jhabvala recalls early years of happiness in Cologne, she rarely speaks of the years 1933 to 1939. In 1933, the year Adolf Hitler and the National Socialists came to power in Germany, Jhabvala, age six, began her education in a segregated Jewish school.[4] It was a world very different from the Germany toward which her mother had felt such a sense of patriotism. Instead of reciting poems for the kaiser's birthday, as her mother had been chosen to do, the young Ruth Prawer ran the daily gauntlet of anti-Semitism that had to be endured by all Jewish children. She recalls signs outside shops and cinemas proclaiming JEWS NOT DESIRED, effectively debarring Jews from entering, and also recalls walking to school past gangs of youths breaking the windows of Jewish-owned shops.[5]

Yet despite the fact that Jhabvala's parents were arrested in 1934, it was some years before her father could persuade his wife to leave Germany. Only in April 1939 did the Prawer family—mother, father, and two children—finally flee; they were among the last Jewish families to escape Hitler's Germany.

But the horrors of Nazi Germany followed them to England. As Jhabvala reminds us, "Everyone knows what happened to German Jews first and other European Jews after. Our family was no exception" ("Disinheritance," 6). She and the members of her immediate family were the only ones to immigrate to England. By the end of the war her father's entire family was dead: "Every last one was killed in a camp. We counted more than 40" ("A Heritage of Lonely Wandering," 7). This terrible loss, together with the reports of how his family died, was too much for Marcus Prawer; in 1948 he committed suicide. Ruth Prawer Jhabvala has never returned to Germany, which for her remains part of a Europe that "now does smell of blood" (Weinraub, 106); nor has she ever written about her childhood there. Since the age of 12, Jhabvala has been ever a foreigner in an adopted home, unable or unwilling to return to the land of her birth.

England

Jhabvala's first adopted home was England. Although her parents had hoped to immigrate to America, problems in obtaining visas in time and the outbreak of war while they were in Britain caused the family to settle in England. They lived first in Coventry (and from here Ruth Prawer and her brother were evacuated to Leamington Spa) and later in Hendon, a London suburb with a large Jewish population, where her parents bought a house and her father started a clothing business.

From an early age Ruth Prawer Jhabvala had begun to write. She remembers her first composition at school in Germany: "The subject: a hare—in German, *der Hase*. I wrote the title, 'Der Hase.' At once I was flooded with my destiny; only I didn't know that's what it was. I only remember my entire absorption, delight, in writing about—giving my impression of—*der Hase*. To think that such happiness could be! ("Disinheritance," 7). Almost as soon as she arrived in England she made an apparently easy transition to writing in English, and about English subjects. It appears that once in England, the young Ruth Prawer deliberately tried to shut out the memory of Germany. In contrast, her brother eagerly studied the German classics, read German at Cambridge, and in time became an authority on Heine. He recently retired from his academic post of Taylor Professor of German Language and Literature at Oxford University. Jhabvala has published only one story, "A Birthday in London" (originally published in the *New Yorker* and included in her first collection of stories, *Like Birds, like Fishes*), that deals with the life she and the other members of her family must have experienced in their early years in Britain, when a lot of Jewish refugees and exiled Poles would visit her father.

Jhabvala was educated at Hendon County School (a local grammar school) and later, between 1945 and 1951, attended Queen Mary College, a college of London University, where she read English literature.

In retrospect she sees this period—during which time she immersed herself in the novels of George Eliot, Thomas Hardy, and Charles Dickens and studied many of the great European classics—as the one in which she acquired the tools of her trade as an author: "This was the great gift, the inheritance, that England gave me: my education which became my tradition—the only tradition I had: that of European literature. It became my equipment, my baggage for the journey I didn't know I had to make: the journey to India" ("Disinheritance," 8). Ruth Prawer became a naturalized British citizen in 1948. Three years later she graduated with an M.A. degree in English literature, having submitted a thesis entitled "The Short Story in England, 1700–1750."

In 1949 she met Cyrus S. H. Jhabvala, an Indian student of architecture, at a party in London. He went back to India but returned in 1951 to marry her. Shortly after graduating from Queen Mary College, Ruth Prawer was married at Burnt Oak register office and left England for India. In his autobiographical work, *The Continent of Circe*, Nirad Chaudhuri, a friend of the Jhabvalas, describes their marriage as "the case of a modern Persian liberating a modern Jewish maiden from her Babylonian exile in London."[6] Once again Jhabvala found herself amid the alien corn.

India

Ruth Prawer Jhabvala never knew the India of the British raj that she writes about in *Heat and Dust*. Nor did she marry into a family that had supported the raj. Her husband's father was a trade-union leader who had spent eight years in prison under the British, and her mother-in-law had been a prominent women's leader (Weinraub, 112). The India Ruth Jhabvala moved to was a newly independent India, full of hope, unlike either the war-torn Britain she had known during her early years in that country or the Britain of postwar rationing she had left in 1951.

The Jhabvalas settled in Delhi, where their three daughters, Renana, Ava, and Firoza, were born and grew up. Jhabvala's early years in India were very different from those an Englishwoman would normally have expected. She met few Europeans and lived a reasonably typical middle-class Indian life. And for almost the first 10 years she was in India Ruth Prawer Jhabvala was in love with everything she saw there: "The smells and sights and sounds of India—the mango and jasmine on hot nights—the rich spiced food—the vast sky—the sight of dawn and dusk—the birds flying about—the ruins—the music" ("Disinheritance," 8). Her early impressions, then, were full of the sensuous beauty she saw all around her in the country she described as a "paradise on earth."[7] And just as on her arrival in Britain she had begun to write exclusively about England and the English, so now she wrote exclusively about India and Indians. Within two years of her arrival in India Jhabvala had completed her first Indian novel, *To Whom She Will*. She sent the manuscript to her mother in England, together with a list of British publishers and the instructions that if one publisher rejected the book, the manuscript was to be sent to the next on the list. It was accepted by Allen and Unwin, the fourth publisher to see the work, and published in the United States by Norton under the title *Amrita*. Jhabvala was immediately hailed as a talented new novelist, was compared with Jane Austen, and was seen to be breaking away from the established style of Indo-Anglian fiction.

By the time *To Whom She Will* was published in 1955, Jhabvala had finished her second novel, *The Nature of Passion*, which again drew praise from the reviewers. Some were amazed that Jhabvala, after only a few years in India, could write about India and Indians so convincingly. In her first two novels all the major characters are Indian, and the subject is the Hindu joint family and arranged marriage versus romantic love. Indeed, the Hindu joint family plays an important part in her first six novels. Although her husband is a Parsi and their domestic situation has never resembled that of the typical Hindu extended family life she portrays in her novels, Jhabvala came to know well the traditional extended family in which her husband's Punjabi partner lived. It is evident that by living with Indians and observing at close quarters the families that lived around her, Jhabvala gained an intimate knowledge of Indian family life, albeit one limited to Delhi's educated, middle-class, primarily Punjabi community, and one limited too by being seen through Western eyes.

Soon after the publication of her second novel Jhabvala began to publish short stories in the *New Yorker*, and for the next 20 years she continued to contribute stories regularly to that magazine.

In 1960 Jhabvala returned to England for the first time. The trip was to have a profound effect on her attitude toward India: "I saw people eating in London, everyone had clothes, and everything in me began to curdle about India."[8] It appears that since her first trip back to England, Jhabvala, like many of her characters, has been "strapped to a wheel" that takes her through the stages she believes all Europeans who visit India go through. She explains these stages in her much-quoted essay "Myself in India," the introduction to her third collection of stories, *An Experience of*

India: "There is a cycle that Europeans—by Europeans I mean all Westerners, including Americans—tend to pass through. It goes like this: first stage, tremendous enthusiasm—everything Indian is marvellous; second stage, everything Indian not so marvellous; third stage, everything Indian abominable. For some people it ends there, for others the cycle renews itself and goes on. I have been through it so many times that now I think of myself as strapped to a wheel that goes round and round and sometimes I'm up and sometimes I'm down."[9]

Her changed attitude is clearly reflected in her fifth novel, *Get Ready for Battle*, in which she confronts head-on the "terrible pressure of poverty and disease" (Mooney, 52) she saw all around her in India. In *Get Ready for Battle* Jhabvala does not pull her punches as she did when she raised the subject of the exploitation of the poor by wealthy and hypocritical businessmen like Lalaji of *The Nature of Passion*. That India's terrible poverty was slowly beginning to overwhelm her and that she undoubtedly felt helpless before it may account for the shift away from purely Indian subjects to an interest in Western, predominantly European characters in all her fiction after *Get Ready for Battle*.

The problems and frustrations experienced by her Western characters reflect her own growing sense of dissatisfaction with her adopted country. In "Myself in India" she candidly describes her life of loneliness and alienation in India:

So I am back again alone in my room with the blinds drawn and the air-conditioner on. Sometimes, when I think of my life, it seems to have contracted to this one point and to be concentrated in this one room, and it is always a very hot, very long afternoon when the air-conditioner has failed. I cannot describe the *oppression* of such afternoons. It is a physical oppression— heat pressing down on me and pressing in the walls and the ceiling and congealing together with time which has stood still and will never move again. And it is not only those two—heat and time—that are laying their weight on me but behind them, or held within them, there is something more which I can only describe as the whole of India. This is hyperbole, but I need hyperbole to express my feelings about those countless afternoons spent over what now seem to me countless years in a country for which I was not born. ("Myself in India," 14)

But although Jhabvala may indeed be an outsider in India, she is undoubtedly, as Ramlal Agarwal aptly expresses in the title of an early essay on her, an "Outsider with Unusual Insight."[10]

Given her unusual background, it is perhaps not surprising that Jhabvala has focused much of her creative writing on the problems of alienation and integration, the problems of strangers in a strange land that have been part of her own experience. However long she remained in India, and despite speaking Hindi and being part of an Indian family, she could never resignedly become Indian. During the 1960s and 1970s the heat and dust of India, the debilitating effect of living alongside poverty she could do nothing to ease, grew harder to bear, and in response Jhabvala attempted to distance herself by spending an increasing amount of time inside her house. But this lack of contact with everyday India presented no difficulties to Jhabvala the writer: "I find I get far more out of going out infrequently than if I went out every day. There are weeks and months when I don't leave the house, but when I do leave it I'm so excited, every sight and sound is like new, and the same with the people."[11]

Ruth Prawer Jhabvala's involvement in film, which began in 1961 when James Ivory and Ishmail Merchant asked her to write a screenplay based on her fourth novel, *The Householder*, has also had a significant effect on her fiction. While all her early novels are set in Delhi, her work for the cinema forced her to travel more and brought her into contact with a greater range of people—though even so, Jhabvala has never been south of Hyderabad and has probably seen less of India than many European travelers. It is interesting to note that the Merchant-Ivory-Jhabvala triumvirate, in their three different backgrounds—Indian, American, and European, respectively—combine the various aspects of Jhabvala's own triple heritage.

Without ever adopting the values of a memsahib (yet never becoming Indian either), Jhabvala has admitted to "a certain nostalgia" for the India of the British raj. This factor, along with her interest in *A Passage to India* that was already evident in *A New Dominion*, may account in part for her decision to write about the past for the first time in her eighth and best-known novel, *Heat and Dust*, which won the Booker Prize, Britain's most prestigious literary award, in 1975.

While writing *Heat and Dust*, her last novel to be set wholly in India, Jhabvala became ill with jaundice—the first endemic Indian disease she contracted in 25 years in that country. This illness, together with her increasing need to withdraw from contemporary India, caused her to leave India and make a new home, once again on foreign soil, in New York.

America

Looking back on her early years in India, Jhabvala speculates that her
Jewish heritage may have eased her passage to India: "Perhaps I loved it
then because of my being Jewish. The Indian family life, the humor was
closer to the Jewish world I knew than the Anglo-Saxon world" ("A
Novelist of India Reflects 2 Worlds," 31). This same Jewish heritage
eased her passage to the United States, a passage her parents had hoped to
make almost 40 years earlier. When she felt the need to leave India, her
choices were limited because she had nowhere to call home. The Germany she left in 1939 was Nazi Germany and she had no desire to return
to the memories of that country; England was where she grew up and
probably more than anywhere else was "home," but it was nevertheless a
home amid the alien corn. Jhabvala explains her move from India to New
York in the following way: "You can't live in a completely alien
place. . . . I got very homesick for Europe. It was a homesickness that
was so terrible, so consuming. And the only place that reminded me of
the Europe that I once knew was New York" (Weinraub, 106). Thus
Jhabvala sees her decision to move to New York, though another foreign
home on another foreign continent, as a return to the Europe of her early
childhood. As she explained in her Neil Gunn Memorial Lecture:

I met the people who should have remained in my life—people I went to school
with in Cologne, with exactly the same background as my own, same heritage,
same parentage. Now here they were living in New York, as Americans, in old
West Side apartments, with high ceilings and heavy furniture, just like the ones
we grew up in in our Continental cities (as blissfully overheated as my grand-
parents' flat in Cologne), and with the delicatessen at the corner selling those
very potato salads and pickled cucumbers and marinated herrings that our
grandmothers used to make. In fact, I haven't had these childhood tastes on my
tongue since I left Germany in 1939—the exact, memory-stirring, awakening,
madeleine taste that magically opens the door into one's personal and ancestral
past. ("Disinheritance," 12)

This is the New York of her first American novel, *In Search of Love and
Beauty*, complete with the people, furniture, smells, and tastes of her
childhood. *In Search of Love and Beauty* is in some ways a cathartic book
that reconciles Jhabvala to a past long submerged. But the reconciliation
with her deeper past does not eliminate from her work the Indian
element acquired over so many more recent years.

During her 25 years in India, Jhabvala emerged as a major novelist of contemporary India. Her move to New York distanced her from the country that had provided her with the fuel for so many novels and stories, but as her latest novel, *Three Continents*, affirms, it did not entirely take away her subject. (Jhabvala still spends most winters in New Delhi with her husband, and frequently he visits her in America.) In *Three Continents* Jhabvala draws together her triple European, Indian, and American heritages and demonstrates that her subject, far from being taken away from her, has in fact been extended, perhaps even enriched, by her move to New York.

However openly Jhabvala has embraced her new homes, the fact that she has lived in four countries on three different continents has inevitably affected her work considerably. She has been forced to write as an outsider, and she has chosen to make her Western characters outsiders too—expatriates like Esmond of *Esmond in India*; refugees like Etta in *A Backward Place*; seekers like Lee of *A New Dominion* or the narrator of *Heat and Dust*, who have both stepped outside the norms of their own American or British societies; and Olivia Rivers of *Heat and Dust*, who steps beyond the borders of the stifling, insular security of the Anglo-Indian society she finds herself part of. In Jhabvala's later novels characters like the homosexual Mark and his adopted sister, the Jewish orphan Natasha, of *In Search of Love and Beauty*, are marginalized characters too, as are the Wishwell twins, Harriet and Michael, in *Three Continents*, even though they are insiders who choose to be outsiders. This marginalization or sense of being an outsider is a reflection of the author's own background, and one she readily admits. There are, she says, always "aspects of myself in everyone that I write about" (Mooney, 52).

Jhabvala's position as an outsider herself has always made her highly conscious of cultural differences and influences, and consequently her novels and stories always force the reader to be aware of and even confront the cultural influences and prejudices Jhabvala exposes. This aspect of her writing is implicit and at times focuses attention on the East-West encounter, manifesting itself in such novels as *Esmond in India* and *A Backward Place*. Like Henry James and E. M. Forster, Jhabvala sees herself as an external observer and makes leading characters in her own image. And like James and Forster, she uses marriage (and love and courtship too) as a major tool for investigating the manners, religion, beliefs, and so on of different classes of societies and of different cultures.

As this biographical outline shows, Ruth Prawer Jhabvala should not be seen as an Indian writer. Her long residence in India does not make her a novelist of that country any more than, say, Kamala Markandaya's long residence in England makes her an English writer. Jhabvala's background makes it equally difficult to see her as either a British writer or an American one. Such speculation is fruitful only to a point, and Jhabvala herself perhaps best describes her ambiguous position: "I write differently from Indian writers because my birth, background, ancestry, and traditions are different. If I must be considered anything, then let it be as one of those European writers who have written about India."[12] It is in this light that I wish to approach Ruth Prawer Jhabvala's fiction.

Chapter Two

India without the Heat and Dust

The Early Indian Novels

Ruth Prawer Jhabvala's first two novels, *To Whom She Will* (1955) and *The Nature of Passion* (1956), share much in common and have many affinities with the early novels of Henry James and all the novels of E. M. Forster. Both books are concerned almost exclusively with Indian characters, both revolve around arranged marriages, both consider aspects of class, and both treat the theme of growth to maturity. Both too are novels of contrast; the modern views of characters like Amrita and Hari in *To Whom She Will* and Viddi and Nimmi in *The Nature of Passion*, for example, are contrasted with the traditional, orthodox views of Sushila's grandmother and Lalaji's sister, Phuphiji. And at the heart of these two novels, at the same time the cause and the solution of many of the conflicts Jhabvala explores, is the traditional Hindu joint family, an extended family that usually comprises at least three generations. It is an institution criticized frequently by the younger members of the various families, Amrita, Viddi, and Nimmi, but rarely by Jhabvala herself, who presents it as an accomplished fact of Indian life. Her descriptions of the tensions and instabilities within the families she portrays suggest that as an outsider she sees that the place of this institution in society is in a state of change. The pictures she presents of Hari being bought by Sushila's family or Kuku being paid for by Nimmi's family are, beneath the surface charm, disturbing ones to a Western observer or to a young Westernized Indian. She is also aware of the shortcomings of romantic love, as Haydn Williams indicates when he writes that Jhabvala "likes to develop plots in which romantic love is less than adequate."[1] The oppressive heat, the smells, and the dirt, so evocatively described in later books, are all but absent in these novels.

The original title of Ruth Prawer Jhabvala's first novel, *To Whom She Will*, comes from a verse in Arthur W. Ryder's translation of the *Panchatantra*, which is used as an epigraph:

For if she bides a maiden still
She gives herself to whom she will;
Then marry her in tender age
So warns the heaven-begotten sage.

Both the title and the epigraph (which is not included in later editions) direct the reader to the plot that revolves around the marriages for Amrita and Hari by their respective families, as well as the plot that concentrates on the relationship between the two young lovers themselves. When the novel was published in the United States the following year (1956), however, the title was changed to *Amrita*. This second title directs the reader away from the theme of arranged marriage versus love marriage and toward the central character, Amrita, and her growth to maturity; it loses, I think, some of the richness of the earlier title. The edition published by Penguin in 1985 uses the original, British title but omits the epigraph, which again suggests that the novel should be seen not simply as a comedy of marriage but also as a novel of growth to maturity.

With Amrita at the center of the novel, Jhabvala plays out a comedy of love that is clearly reminiscent of her literary predecessor, Jane Austen, a novelist with whom she has frequently, and justifiably, been compared. At the very heart of this comedy of love are the contrasts between the families of the young lovers—Hari's typically lower-middle-class , boistrous Punjabi family, whose members were forced to move to Delhi when the Indian subcontinent was divided into two countries, India and Pakistan, and Amrita's upper-middle-class, long-established Delhi family, which prospered under the British raj and lost nothing with the birth of an independent India.

Jhabvala has used the structure of the novel to emphasize the contrasts between the two families. For much of the novel the chapters alternate between one that is concerned with Amrita's family and one in which a similar scene is played out in Hari's family circle. Jhabvala returns to this structure in *A Backward Place*, in which the three major characters, Judy, Etta, and Clarissa, are contrasted by similar means.

Many of the contrasts in *To Whom She Will* can be seen through the novelist's often-comic portrayal of the mealtimes and eating habits of the various characters. (A list of recipes is even included at the end of the Allen and Unwin edition of the novel.) This interest in food and mealtimes is a means of giving her novels a distinctly Indian identity, at least for the Western reader. The opening chapter of the novel brings Amrita's family together at her grandfather's table. The atmosphere is imposing, even intimidating, and the meal takes place in near silence, as the Rai Bahadur,[2] Amrita's Anglophile grandfather, does not encourage idle conversation: "The dining-room was also furnished in oppressive Victorian style. The dark curtains were drawn to shut out the sun. The silver shone dully. The broad heavy dining-table, with the legs carved into lions' heads, was spread with a gleaming white cloth and laid with initialled cutlery. The servants moved noiselessly over the marble floor, filling up the water glasses and holding the trays with food for the diners to serve themselves."[3] In this passage (which is very like a passage from an early James or Forster novel) the setting is clearly European in both style and formality, and the heavy curtains drawn against the sun shut out not only the harsh light but India too.

In contrast, the second chapter introduces the reader to Hari's family, again as a meal is being eaten. On this occasion, though, Hari, the man of the house, eats alone and is served by his mother: "Hari sat in the courtyard on a charpoy, eating his dinner. He ate gram and vegetables and curds out of little brass bowls on a tray, and his mother kept bringing him freshly made chapatis with which he shovelled up his food. She watched him, saying 'Eat, son, eat.' She was a short, healthy old woman, dressed in a white cotton sari which she wore pulled over her head" (*TWSW*, 11). This meal is very distinctly Indian: the brass bowls on a tray take the place of the well-laid table and gleaming white tablecloth; the *chapatis* substitute for the initialed cutlery; the food is served to Hari by his mother, rather than by a host of smartly dressed servants; and the silence and dimness are replaced by the loud noises that surround Hari as he eats in the open courtyard.

It is this "Indianness" and imagined simplicity that attracts the romantic side of Amrita and endears Hari to her, as can be seen as the two have lunch together in the radio station canteen:

Their lunch arrived and Hari at once began to eat. Amrita was not hungry; and anyway, it was enough for her to watch him eat. She always liked to watch him over his meals; he ate with such relish and with such unselfconscious enjoyment. He handled knife and fork rather awkwardly, which was another thing she found charming about him. He was simple and unspoilt, and his ways the traditional, truly Indian ways which had been lost in her family. She now rather despised her family's sophisticated, highly westernized way of living and thought of it as being false and unreal and quite unsuitable. Some time ago, shortly after she had first met Hari, she had tried to revolt against this way of living and had started to eat with her fingers at home. But her mother had become so indignant, and Krishna Sen Gupta so amused, that she had had to give it up. Once, also, she had asked Hari, why he did not always eat with his hands when he was with her, as he was accustomed to do; but this too had not been a success. Hari had been shocked and rather hurt; to him it had seemed as if she were suggesting he did not know how a gentleman should behave. (*TWSW*, 23)

Rather than drawing the couple together, scenes like this emphasize the gaps between the way Amrita and Hari think and the fundamental differences that exist between the two, differences their families are aware of from the start. Jhabvala repeatedly shows Amrita loving in Hari the things he tries to hide from her, and Hari loving in Amrita the things she is ashamed of in herself. In effect, each is ashamed of his of her class before the other. It is perhaps not so much Hari that Amrita is in love with as the Indianness she thinks she admires in him—an element she sees as vital and full of life—and, of course, in her romantic way she idealizes the very idea of being in love. As Yasmine Gooneratne has pointed out, it is ironic that this "quest for 'Indianness' . . . leads her to Hari's elder sister Prema, in whom she will only discover the familiar combination of wealth and ostentation, together with a new kind of emptiness."[4] The real gap between Hari and Amrita can be seen as the two meet, supposedly to plan their elopement to England, again over a meal:

"All we really have to do," Amrita was saying, "is book our tickets. What else is there?"
"What else," he echoed, trying to identify the smell: could it be oven-baked fish, his favourite dish? (*TWSW*, 144)

The pattern of juxtaposing an event within one family circle with a similar event within the other family circle continues throughout the novel, with the exception of the occasional chapters in which members of the two families meet, the few though important chapters that are concerned with Krishna Sen Gupta, and the chapters that focus on Amrita and Hari themselves. Only in the final chapter does Jhabvala brings all her characters together for a happy conclusion.

The plot of the novel, then, progresses along two distinct lines. The first, which is tied to the theme of marriage, is the thread that follows the plans being made for the young couple by their respective families, both of whom disapprove of the love match they see as unsuitable. The second, which centers on Amrita's growth to maturity, is the thread that follows Hari's and Amrita's affections for each other. The combination of these two threads, which wind around each other, adds real interest and depth to the story. Jhabvala has used this pattern of contrast not only for the obvious purpose of comedy but also to highlight some of the differences between traditional and modern values, between Eastern and Western modes of life, and, significantly, between social classes. Amrita's mother, Radha, who ironically married a man of her own choosing from a very different social background, lectures her daughter on this point: "in marriage the most important thing is that husband and wife should come from the same social class. Of course we are very modern in our family and are not so strict about community and caste; but the class, my loveliest, is still very important, and you cannot be happy if you marry into a family that is not so good as yours" (*TWSW*, 200).

Central to both themes of the novel is the relationship between Amrita and Hari, which is presented as less than adequate from the outset. From the first meeting between the two Hari is shown to be vague about his love for Amrita and always ready to turn his attention to a menu or to his friends. His lack of any real love for Amrita is clearly shown after his first meeting with Sushila: "He only wanted to go home, away from the smiling Mrs. Anand, to lie down on his charpoy and think, just before going to sleep, of Amrita, as he had trained himself to do" (*TWSW*, 40). Although he tries hard to think only of Amrita, his thoughts, vaguely sensual in nature, keep turning to Sushila. Amrita, however, despite her "instinctive unease at . . . loving a young man of her own accord and against her family's wishes" (*TWSW*, 22), is determined to love Hari and is prepared to rebel against her mother and grandfather. And this is just the point; she is prepared to rebel, by loving Hari, by venturing to eat at home with her fingers, and by opposing the will of not only her mother, Radha, but also her grandfather, the patriarchal Rai Bahadur Tara Chand.

We have seen enough of the Rai Bahadur, however, to know that although he perceives himself as a man of liberal views who is "not hidebound" (*TWSW*, 7) by traditional ideas, he is above all else a snob, and his humiliating treatment of Hari illustrates this trait. It is the sterile respectability of her family that Amrita rebels against when she fancies herself in love with Hari, and it is not because of the efforts of her family that she comes to see Hari in a different light as the novel progresses. Where earlier she could ignore or forgive all his foibles and vagueness and think only "about how much she loved him" (*TWSW*, 22), she later views him through slightly different eyes: "She stopped still and looked at him searchingly. It seemed strange to her that he should not understand" (*TWSW*, 76). And as she continues toward maturity, so her understanding of Hari (and of her true feeling for him) grows: "She shut her eyes and said, 'You are thinking only of your oven-baked fish,' and was promptly surprised at herself" (*TWSW*, 145). Similarly, as her understanding of Hari grows, so too does her ability to see others clearly. When Vazir Dayal, her uncle, suggests to Amrita that she should marry Hari regardless of her family's wishes, she knows that his words "were spoken not out of interest for her welfare" (*TWSW*, 72), which implies that she is also beginning to appreciate that the rest of her family, in opposing her proposed marriage to Hari, are acting out of a genuine interest for her welfare, though some time elapses before she is ready to admit this even to herself. Her acceptance of the realization that her family does have her best interests at heart is only acknowledged as she gradually comes to admit that she doesn't love Hari, and these are important stages on Amrita's path to maturity. This theme is central to the novel, while the theme of arranged marriage is used to provide depth, to give Amrita a cause to rebel, and to enhance the comedy. In making arranged marriage a theme of the novel Jhabvala is not simply endorsing the idea unreservedly, though it may still be the best way in the society she portrays. True, the novel ends with the prospect of two happy, apparently arranged marriages, but we should not lose sight of the fact that, ironically, Hari had shown an interest in Sushila Anand before any discussion between his and Sushila's families had taken place, and Amrita and Krishna have effectively chosen each other before Radha makes any definite plans in that direction. The reader is aware all along that Amrita and Krishna are destined for each other. As Linda Warley has observed, a scene early in the novel makes this clear: "Amrita leant her head against the anti-burglar bars and felt happy, because today she was going to see Hari. She could hear her mother shouting at the servant in the kitchen and Krishna Sen Gupta in the bathroom singing under the shower. Today, she thought, I shall see him, another three, four, hours and I shall see him, and she hummed in tune with Krishna Sen Gupta" (*TWSW*, 17). Amrita may consciously be thinking about Hari, but her subconscious thoughts, here and throughout the novel, are in tune with Krishna Sen Gupta rather than with Hari.[5]

Much has been made of Ruth Prawer Jhabvala's presentation of Indians and of the Indian character. European and American critics have tended to see her as an insider and have accepted her views as such, while in India critics have tended to view her as an outsider who does not truly understand India and Indians. In discussions of these early novels the controversy over Jhabvala's portrayal of India and Indians has not reached the passionate levels that a novel like *Heat and Dust* has inspired, but a few passages are of interest nevertheless. Early in the novel Hari is presented in a manner that could be considered patronizing. As Amrita waits for the ever-late Hari, she explains, with what must be seen as the backing of the authorial voice, that "He was delightfully unpractical, so truly Indian, so unworldly, that he could not think of hard-set European things like time and clocks" (*TWSW*, 21). While Jhabvala appears to be suggesting that a true Indian is necessarily unpractical and unpunctual, we must remember that alongside the authorial voice is that of Amrita, who thinks she is in love with Hari and, naively, with his Indianness. Thus the view of the unpractical/unpunctual Indian can also be seen as the upper-middle-class Indian view of the lower classes.

Certainly at this early stage in her writing career Jhabvala was in love with all she saw around her, and India is presented in a somewhat idealized fashion. Amrita's shopping trip to Connaught Place with her mother and the trip to the railway station to see Krishna off are both described with obvious delight, but they are balanced by the poverty the author depicts when, for example, Hari walks between his home and his sister Prema's house:

In his own street, the houses still looked yellow, the plaster crumbling off only in places, and the road still relatively clean; but in the street around the corner, though it had been constructed at the same time, respectability had already degenerated. The houses oozed brown wounds and bulged out of doors and windows with children and washing and jutting ends of furniture. Banana-peels, tomato-skins and rotting bits of vegetable lay squashed in the dust, sniffed by skinny pariah-dogs. On a waste patch, tiny low huts made of mud and old planks of wood had sprung up, stuffed with too many women and too many children, old rags, newspapers, worn-out blankets and discarded tins. (*TWSW*, 13)

Similarly, the author's romanticized portrait of Hindu family life is tinged by her awareness of the tensions of community living in Delhi's crowded quarters, as she shows when Hari's family visit the Anands: "Suddenly from the veranda two floors below came an uproar of voices. Women shrilled and children howled and men boomed with anger. It was one of those family quarrels, sister-in-law against sister, wife against brother-in-law, grandmother against everybody, the tension of community living bursting into a sudden climax which had to rage itself out before it could sink back into the calm of everyday subdued resentment" (*TWSW*, 123).

Jhabvala may have chosen not to write about the harsher realities of everyday life in India, as she has every right to do, but she is not unaware of them. Some of these realities are voiced through Dr. Mukherji, who makes her only, fleeting appearance over a meal at the home of Tarla, Amrita's aunt. The practical Dr. Mukherji, who apparently embodies the best of East and West in her religious principles and her knowledge of the modern discipline of economics, is a welcome contrast to the other committee women seen in this and later novels; Tarla Mathur and Lady Ram Prashad Khanna are the first in a long line of "dedicated social workers" satirized by the author in her novels. Dr. Mukherji is the only one who sees beyond the paperwork and the endless women's committees to the real problems of village life: "'And also,' Dr. Mukherji dropped in, speaking in a very low voice, not caring whether anyone heard her or not, 'village women in labour, with the female scavenger standing by with a piece of glass to cut the navel cord'" (*TWSW*, 30). Her only other contribution to the mealtime conversation adds a jarring note to the topic of marriage: "'Last week,' she said, 'my sweeper's daughter was married. She is twelve'" (*TWSW*, 32). Her remarks are all the more poignant for the way they are politely ignored by the others. It is perhaps a shame that Dr. Mukherji (who is something of an avatar of Dr. Prance in Henry James's *The Bostonians*—a wonderful woman doctor with a small but strong role) plays so minor a part in this novel, but a similar character is developed more fully in Sarla Devi of *Get Ready for Battle.*

Professor Hoch, whose appearance is equally fleeting, is in comparison an amusing if somewhat ridiculous figure who has set himself up as an expert on India. He is the only significant European character to appear in the first two novels, but his brief appearance shows that Jhabvala is very aware of one type of European who inhabits India, and again, a comparable character is developed in Esmond of *Esmond in India*. Perhaps surprisingly, Jhabvala appears to view Professor Hoch through Indian rather than Western eyes. Like so many of Jhabvala's minor characters, Dr. Mukherji and Professor Hoch make a definite impression on the reader and provide early proof of the writer's mastery of portraiture and an economy of style reminiscent of Jane Austen.

Characters like Dr. Mukherji show that Jhabvala disapproves of those who shut out the harsher reality of Indian life, even though that reality can at times be difficult to deal with. Thus authorial censure is directed toward the Rai Bahadur for this very reason. In the opening chapter we learn that his "dark curtains were drawn to shut out the sun" (*TWSW*, 9). And later this censure is applied even more forcefully, when the Rai Bahadur is seen to be quite deliberately shutting out what he does not wish to see: "And he saw, or perhaps only guessed at, disturbing visions of a life outside his house, of real round figures agitating black and solid in a rhythm which he did not understand; and with Amrita among them, accepting this strange rhythm, denying his own. It was an intolerable vision, and with an effort of will he shut it out" (*TWSW*, 174–75.) Another member of Amrita's family, her aunt Tarla, is also censured for the same reason: "All the curtains were drawn, shutting out the sun, shutting out the life of the exhausted city" (*TWSW*, 68). Tarla and her fellow committee women gather to discuss the problems of India, yet ironically, as Jhabvala shows through the Jamesian image of the closed curtains that shut out life, they cut themselves off from and refuse to see those very problems. Amrita, unlike her grandfather or her aunt, makes no attempt to shut out the real India; her problem in the early stages of the story is that she embraces it with romantic arms. Later she begins to realize that while her family's attitudes have been wrong, so too have aspects of her own. She will still see India with open eyes and through open blinds but without the rose-tinted spectacles that colored her earlier, romantic view.

Marriage again plays an important role in *The Nature of Passion*, but the central focus of Ruth Prawer Jhabvala's second novel is expounded in the title and the epigraph from which it is taken:

Know thou Rajas to be of the nature of passion, giving rise to thirst (for pleasure) and attachment. It binds the embodied by attachment to action.

This epigraph, from the *Bhagavad Gita*, XIV, 7 (translated by Swami Paramananda), is accompanied by a commentary from Dr. Radhakrishnan:

The three modes are present in all human beings, though in different degrees. No one is free from them and in each soul one or the other predominates. Men are said to be sattvika, rajasa or tamasa according to the mode which prevails . . . While the activities of a sattvika temperament are free, calm and selfless, the rajasa nature wishes to be always active and cannot sit still and its activities are tainted by selfish desires.

Lala Narayan Dass Verma (Lalaji, as he is known), the superbly drawn central character of the novel, is a *rajasa*, and his is the nature of passion referred to in the title, which undoubtedly has further, intentional ambiguity. During the course of the novel we see Lalaji following his nature and pursuing his tainted activities and selfish desires, though not infrequently with a twinge of conscience. Contrasting with Lalaji is his aged clerk, who freely quotes from the *Upanishads* and the *Gita* and who, although he works for Lalaji, keeps himself apart from his employer's corrupt business practices. This clerk, who acts as a foil to his avaricious employer, provides the words that comfort Lalaji when his conscience pricks him:

> Once his clerk had explained to him that every man is born with a certain nature, and that it is his task in life to act according to that nature. "Man attains perfection," he had quoted, "being engaged in his own duty. He who does the duty born of his own nature incurs no sin." This information had been very interesting to Lalaji, for he had construed from it that it was not the desire for money or for power that had driven him on, but the nature with which he had been born. He had been endowed with the nature of a rich man, this he clearly understood: hence it had been his duty to *make* himself a rich man. In his pursuit of wealth he had only been following the path of his duty; he had done as God meant him to do, he had done well.[6]

This passage is full of irony because Lalaji bends or misrepresents (perhaps unconsciously) the words of his clerk. Even when he hears wise words, Lalaji is capable of hearing in them what he wishes to hear.

Money, then, is the ruling passion in this book, and through money and their attitude toward it, the various characters of the novel are examined and exposed.

Lalaji, despite his obvious avarice, is a character the reader feels sympathy for, primarily because of the sincere love he displays for all the members of his family without exception, even for his daughter-in-law Kanta, who makes little attempt to hide her dislike for most of her husband's family, including Lalaji: "She was his son's wife, she had borne his son's children, and even though she came from a different community and her ways were not their ways, he had always tried to love her as a daughter" (*NOP*, 144). The reader also feels sympathy for Lalaji because he recognizes that money in itself does not bring him happiness: "He knew that money and power were ultimately worthless and had no meaning" (*NOP*, 176). He also realizes that he was happier when he had no wealth and lived with his family in two rooms, yet ironically his love for his family often manifests itself only through money.

Rani and Om Prakash, Lalaji's eldest daughter and son, grew up in less opulent surroundings than the family now enjoys, and their upbringing was very traditional—neither was well educated, and marriages were arranged for both at an early age. As was natural, Om brought his wife, Shanta, to live in his father's household, while Rani went to live with her husband's family. Because they grew up observing traditional ways and because they were not highly educated, Rani and Om share views similar to their parents'. As a result, Om had no qualms about accepting a large salary and a place in his father's business, and Rani is proud of Lalaji's success and of his money. There are, of course, some differences between Lalaji and his two eldest children—Om, for example, does not appear to have inherited his father's unmeasured love for his family. But neither Om nor Rani has moved away from Lalaji in the way his other children have; they have the money but not the manners or education to enable them to move up in class. Through Lalaji and his children Jhabvala demonstrates that different times and cultures produce different vices. Lalaji's early poverty produces the money fever of his later life, while Om's upbringing in changing times produces other errors, and so with Lalaji's other children too.

Chandra Prakash was the first of Lalaji's children to enjoy the benefits of his father's newly acquired wealth: "At the time, fourteen years ago, he [Lalaji] had not been a rich man for very long and so had wanted all the things a rich man traditionally has—including an England-returned son" (*NOP*, 81). But Chandra returned home a different person, with modern, independent ideas, and instead of joining his father's business as Om had done, he took a job as a gazetted government officer and, despite the strong disapproval of his family, married a girl of his own choosing from outside their community. Because of Lalaji's money (which was an important factor in Chandra's being accepted by Kanta's family) and because of the education that money had provided, Chandra Prakesh has been able to move to a higher class, a movement that will be cemented in his children. Because of this perceived upward move, Chandra is ashamed of his family, and Kanta wants nothing to do with them. To highlight this snobbery Jhabvala makes much of the couple's dependence on Lalaji's money; Kanta's words are typical of their attitude toward him: " 'It is terrible to be related to such a man. I wish we need have nothing to do with him.' But this she knew was impossible. There were so many things they needed and which could not be managed on Chandra's salary. She especially looked forward to her holiday in the hills every summer. 'He is your father, we owe him some respect'" (*NOP*, 116).

Both Chandra and Kanta show that they understand the passion for money, even if they do not like it. Lalaji's experience with Chandra Prakash has convinced him that one England-returned son is enough, and while both Ved Prakesh (Viddi) and Nimmi are college educated, he has no intention of allowing Viddi to go to England to continue his studies. For this reason Viddi is rebelling against his family and refusing to join his father's business, imagining himself instead a great patron of the arts—rather like the young man Krishna meets in *To Whom She Will* when he visits Calcutta, the young man who is so obviously satirized by Jhabvala and scorned by Krishna. Viddi can afford to do this, of course, because he has never known what it is to be without money. His reason for despising the family business is entirely selfish, and his scornful attitude stems from reasons very different from those which might cause characters like Krishna Sen Gupta in *To Whom She Will* or Sudhir Banerjee in *A Backward Place* to feel scorn for the business of a man like Lalaji. Viddi, who professes to scoff at money—"'Money, money, money,' he said. "That is all anyone thinks of in this house'" (*NOP*, 15)—spends his time wandering in and out of coffeehouses complaining to anyone who will listen how his father will not give him any money. Viddi, Jhabvala shows, may scorn money, but he desperately wants all the things that money can buy. Ironically, he expects his impoverished friends to be sympathetic to his complaints:

"You do not know how I suffer at home. Not one of them understands me. They cannot understand what it is I want, for they think that the only thing one can want is money."

Zahir-ud-din sighed wistfully: he wanted money very badly. It was true that he wanted to be a famous artist, but above all he wanted to be a rich one. (*NOP*, 32–33)

Viddi fails to understand that the desire for money is, in varying degrees, almost universal (Esmond clearly expresses it in *Esmond in India*). While Viddi may feel badly done by at home, the reader knows just how well he is fed and how comfortable he really is; Zahir-ud-din, by contrast, has a wife and three children whom he can barely support. Viddi does, however, gradually become sensible to the passion for money and in so doing is able to see his coffeehouse friends in their true light: "Much as he valued their friendship, Viddi began to doubt whether they felt as deeply for him as he did for them. It seemed almost as if the beauty of his friendship was of less consequence to them than his father's money" (*NOP*, 94–95).

Lalaji, who sees the desire for money as the proper instinct of man, has always recognized the value of money and quite deliberately uses it as the carrot to bring Viddi back into the family fold and into the family business: "Let him have his 500 rupees a month. After three months of it, he would start him on the sweepers' hutments and give him a salary of 800 rupees a month; and by that time he trusted Viddi would have learnt the value of money—how much better 800 rupees is than 500, 1,000 rupees than 800, 2,000 rupees than 1,000—and would adjust his ideas accordingly." (*NOP*, 98). And Lalaji is soon proved correct. Viddi will take his place in the family business and in time will become quite like Om, as Ruth Prawer Jhabvala suggests in the closing lines of the novel: "Shanta looked up and for a moment she thought Viddi was her husband, he looked so much like him; even his voice, it seemed to her, sounded like Om's" (*NOP*, 192).

Nimmi, like her brother Viddi, also professes a lack of interest in money: "Pitaji, you think you can buy everything with money" (*NOP*, 15), she remarks casually to her father, desiring to suggest the contrary where she is concerned. Yet though she may realize that money alone cannot bring her the things she wants, she fails to understand how much she relies on the money she so easily dismisses as unimportant. Like Viddi, Nimmi may think she does not value money, but everything she enjoys—her fine clothes, her secret trips to the club with her friend Rajen—and everything she hopes to enjoy in the future—trips abroad, a fashionable life-style—depend on it. Like Viddi, Nimmi too comes to realize the value of money as she tells Rajen about the marriage that has been arranged for her, and they consider how she can avoid what they regard as a terrible fate:

"You can go to stay in a hotel. Only you must not give your real name. Then if people read your family's advertisement in the newspaper, nobody will know it is you."

"I have no money to go to a hotel, it is very costly. You know I have only my allowance and I spend it all."

"Always money," Rajen said with a sigh, and Nimmi sighed in unison.

Hitherto money had been for her merely something of which her father had plenty. (*NOP*, 181)

It is only at this point that Nimmi comprehends the full implications of Lalaji's money: "Perhaps until now she had not fully understood herself how much, how completely, she belonged to her family"(*NOP*, 182). Like her brothers Chandra and Viddi, Nimmi comes to appreciate the value of money, and is forced to accept her family ties, which she perceives as being particularly restrictive for a young woman.

But the reader already knows who Nimmi's husband is going to be, and we therefore cannot share her fears or horror of arranged marriage. As she did in *To Whom She Will*, Jhabvala appears to present arranged marriage in a favorable light. Both Rani and Om Prakesh have had marriages arranged for them by their family, and despite Om's obvious shortcomings his wife, Shanta, is shown to be happy both with Om as a husband and in her father-in law's household. We know too that Nimmi's marriage to the fashionable Kuku, whose background parallels her own and whose modern ideas suit hers, will be a happy one. Like Amrita, Nimmi had wanted to choose her own husband and had imagined herself married to her obviously dull Parsi boyfriend, Pheroze Batliwala. But just as Amrita came to realize she didn't love Hari and that her true feelings were for Krishna Sen Gupta, so Nimmi awakens to the fact that Pheroze does not really interest her, and the way is open for her affections to be transferred to Kuku: "It was strange, Nimmi thought, but when she was away from Pheroze she was more excited about him than she generally was when she was with him" (*NOP*, 131). Nimmi, like Chandra Prakesh, will move in circles very different from those of the rest of her family when she marries Kuku; unlike her brother, however, she will not alienate herself from her family. Yet this aspect of the novel is not wholly satisfactory. As Haydn Williams has commented, "we feel somewhat cheated when we discover that Kuku is all along the husband chosen by Dev Raj for Nimmi."[7] Such a "shock denouement," as Williams calls it, is somewhat out of place, and it is not as smoothly handled as Amrita's discovery that she loves Krishna Sen Gupta, an outcome Jhabvala had hinted at throughout *To Whom She Will*. Nonetheless, any misgivings about the ending should not be allowed to cloud the Austenish pleasure of the overall novel and its wonderful and at-times satiric depiction of a Hindu family.

While both Nimmi and Viddi, in the early stages of the novel, loudly voice their disdain of Lalaji's wealth, their sister Usha is the sole member of the family who genuinely has no interest in money and who ironically is seen as stupid by everyone, including herself. She thinks of nothing but marriage and the prospect of having babies of her own and is thoroughly happy at the thought of her forthcoming marriage.

Chandra Prakesh, the only one of Lalaji's children to have married outside his own community, is seen as happy enough, but his relationship with his family is strained and always will be. Although he has married independently and has a job outside the family business, he is still forced to turn to his family for money, and this factor contributes greatly to his unhappiness—of all Lalaji's children, Chandra is the only one who will never be wholly contented. Yet even he is forced to toe the family line when he is persuaded by Lalaji to hand over the incriminating letter in the government's file on the T—— bribery case.

The conflicts that arise in the novel—which in Nimmi's case appear to be related to marriage and in Viddi's case appear to stem from his desire to go to England rather than enter the family business (and Chandra, of course, had both studied abroad and married a girl of her own choosing)—are all caused by different ways of seeing money. This aspect is perhaps most clearly suggested by Nimmi's response to her cousin Lakshmi's use of the term *rich*: "Nimmi knew what the other girl meant by rich. Their own families were rich too, in terms of money, probably a good deal more so than those of Rajen and Indira—but only in terms of money. What Lakshmi meant was that the parents of Rajen and Indira were very modern and advanced, had been educated in England, gave dinners to exclusive people and went to garden-parties at Rashtrapati Bhavan. But because she was a crude uncultured girl she used the word 'rich'" (*NOP*, 47). There are two ways in which the word *rich* is used in this novel—in terms of money and in terms of culture. For Lalaji, and for Om and Rani, it can mean only financial wealth. As Lalaji's wife thought, "what was the use of so much wealth if all it did for you was to force you to abandon your own comfortable habits" (*NOP*, 18). For Chandra, Viddi, and Nimmi, however, wealth enables them to throw off those "comfortable habits" and embrace a culture they see as modern and advanced. Thus the different ways of seeing money ultimately cause the divisions between them and their family and places them in a different social class. It is perhaps a sad reflection on the India Jhabvala presents in this novel that behind the obvious vitality and appeal of her characters lie selfishness and corruption—from businessmen to government officers, even to the would-be artists in the coffee shops.

Both these early novels are concerned almost exclusively with Indian characters, and Jhabvala approaches her themes, as far as possible, from Indian angles. This element is shown even in the titles, which suggest that Jhabvala is attempting to approach subjects of universal appeal from Indian viewpoints. The interest in the marriage market in both novels calls to mind the novels of Jane Austen as well as those of Henry James and E. M. Forster (who also progress via Jane Austen); the interest in money and the apparent difficulty in understanding wealth in *The Nature of Passion* also recall the novels of those writers, particularly Austen's *Pride and Prejudice* and the wonderful opening paragraph of *Mansfield Park*. And like Jane Austen's work, Jhabvala's scope, especially in these two novels, is limited—not to "3 or 4 families in a country village" but to three or four families in Delhi. Like Jane Austen, Jhabvala sets the action of her novels predominantly within or around the households of the families she treats, and excursions into Delhi, like Austen's excursions to such places as Bath, London, and Portsmouth, are rare.

While Professor Hoch is the only European who has a real part in Jhabvala's first two novels, he is not the only European mentioned. In *The Nature of Passion* Nimmi's attention is drawn to a European woman at the club, whom Rajen tells her is Frau Kunz, "the wife of someone from the German Embassy" (*NOP*, 72), where her parents attend parties. At this early stage Jhabvala's foreigners were predominantly German, perhaps reflecting her own heritage. The only other Europeans mentioned are the American singer whom Hari and Amrita watch perform Schubert songs for All-India Radio and the violinist who performs at the Cavalier in *To Whom She Will*, and the bandleader in *The Nature of Passion* who is performing at the nightclub Viddi visits in the company of Kuku. Kuku explains to Viddi that this man "has been in India twenty-five years and now he wants to go home, but he has no money" (*NOP*, 142). As Yasmine Gooneratne has observed, the bandleader is the second in what in Jhabvala's fiction is to be a long line of displaced Westerners who are desperately trying to make the best of their lives in India (Gooneratne, 62–63, 86). In her next novel, *Esmond in India*, Jhabvala makes such a character the center of her novel, and such figures continue to be seen in later works—Etta in *A Backward Place*, for example, and many of the characters in the short stories.

The feasting that is evident at every stage of *To Whom She Will* and that is used there to highlight the contrasts between Hari's and Amrita's families, and to draw attention to the two lovers' unsuitability for each other is used in Jhabvala's second novel to emphasize the solid, middle-class success and comfort of Lalaji and his family. The sheer size of both

Lalaji—whose "immense amount of flesh" (*NOP*, 105) bulges over the sides of his deck chair—and his sons Om and Viddi is testament to their wealth: Rani too is of abundant size; her bosom is described as "ample" and her face as "rather too plump" (*NOP*, 159), reminding us of Mira in *To Whom She Will*, who is "very fat and very soft" (*TWSW*, 8). When Lalaji and Dev Raj meet to discuss Nimmi's proposed marriage, Dev Raj looks approvingly at the size of his granddaughter: "'She is getting fat,' Dev Raj said, looking down with approval at his granddaughter. And Lalaji, also looking at her with a tender smile on his face, replied, 'What else, pure ghee we give her every day and chicken curry,' which made them laugh a lot" (*NOP*, 105). Lalaji is only half-joking. Both Dev Raj and Lalaji see a large feast or a fat baby as a reflection of their success.

One rarely discussed aspect of these novels is their sense of history and politics. Like all Jhabvala's novels with the exception of the earlier story in *Heat and Dust*, *To Whom She Will* and *The Nature of Passion* are set in the period in which they were written. Thus while her novels are not "historical" or "political" in any generally accepted sense, the presence of the politics of the time—the recent struggle for independence and the terrible months of Partition—is nevertheless evident. Though the sense of history is by no means as strong in these novels as in *A New Dominion* and particularly *Heat and Dust*, there are still many references to recent political or historical events. Memories of the British raj and, more important, of Partition are never far away in *To Whom She Will*, which was first published only eight years after the division of the subcontinent. Hari's family are Punjabi refugees who came to Delhi at the time of Partition:

Hari Sahni's family was a large and widespread one. They were Punjabi Hindus who in 1947, at the time of the Partition, had to leave their native Lahore, which they incorporated into Pakistan, and fly to Delhi. They had lost almost everything; their houses, their business, many of their valuables, all had to be left behind. It was complete disaster, absolute ruin: if it had happened to one man alone it would have been unbearable. But there is consolation in numbers, and there were hundreds of thousands of them. Their relatives, their friends, their neighbours, all were ruined with them, all had to start life afresh: there was no individual disgrace attached to this ruin; it was spiritually bearable. And like almost all Punjabis, they were resourceful, courageous, intensely practical people who faced their situation squarely: there was no help for it, and they had to earn their living; so they started again. They did not care how small or humble were their beginnings, and they worked hard. Within three or four years they

were almost where they had been before, and some of them had even bettered
themselves. (*TWSW*, 34)

As an account of the political history of the recent past, this is obviously
perfunctory, but it does successfully illustrate the way in which the
fortunes of families like Hari's have been shaped by the horrendous
events that accompanied India's freedom. And in Amrita's family too
there are constant reminders of earlier days, this time of the freedom
struggle that Amrita's father, Nirad Chakravarty, had embraced whole-
heartedly. Memories of the struggle for independence still cover the
walls of Radha's house:

In the place of honour, on the wall facing Amrita's painting, was a coloured one
of Gandhiji, smiling in blue; beside, above, and beneath it were photographs of
Amrita's father, Nirad Chakravarty: Nivad Chakravarty as a young lawyer, very
thin and earnest in a tight-fitting European suit with a high collar and a book
under his arm; Nirad Chakravarty, still thinner and more earnest but now
wearing only white khadi clothes, on the outskirts of a group of prominent
Congress personalities; Nirad Chakravarty on a platform, addressing a meeting;
Nirad Chakravarty one of a group around Gandhiji himself; and the last picture
taken in 1944 just after he came out of jail at the expiration of his last sentence,
alone in a garden chair, a little dim, death foreshadowed in the blurred
photograph. (*TWSW*, 17)

And even as Hari is being married, his mind wanders back to the time
when "his father had held him up on his shoulder to see Gandhiji, just
out of prison, smiling" (*TWSW*, 233).

In *The Nature of Passion* reference is made to the time when "the stream
of Hindu refugees had come pouring into Delhi from the Punjab" (*NOP*,
40). But Lalaji's sympathy for these refugees is limited by his own success
and by his own personal view of Punjabis: "in reality he did not feel much
sympathy. It was seven years now since the refugees had come to Delhi,
and he considered that any Punjabi worth the name should by this time
have re-established himself" (*NOP*, 42). More poignantly, though, Partition has separated Lalaji from his roots. When troubled by business
matters, Lalaji's thoughts still turn to retirement, to withdrawal, and to
returning to his native village: "For this was the ideal which every man
looked forward to during all his working life: the return to the native village,
the ultimate peace. Yet even this was denied him: his native village in the
Punjab had been incorporated into Pakistan and the ancestral strip of land
was lost to him and his. The only home he had now was in the city, if a home

in the city could be called a home. He had to die there because, like any outcast, he had nowhere to go back to" (*NOP*, 177).

Lalaji's wealth can buy much, and it can do much for his children, who in time will move up the social ladder their father has no wish to climb himself, but behind his wealth is the sadness caused by the knowledge of what he has lost, which is of infinitely more value to one aspect of his character. And like *To Whom She Will*, *The Nature of Passion* ends with more feasting, as Lalaji's family gathers to celebrate Nimmi's coming marriage. But as in the earlier novel, Jhabvala does not overlook the poor and the squalor of India. Here she contrasts the rich feasting of Lalaji and his family with another reality facing the vast majority of the country's population—"In the distance, out on the barren plains, the broken flight of steps of a vanished palace led to nowhere and a man with a stick and a loincloth walked behind two yoked and shabby bullocks" (*NOP*, 190)— and in so doing shows what an incredibly mixed thing "reality" is.

Krishna Sen Gupta in *To Whom She Will* stands alone in these first two novels as a character who finds himself disenchanted with the country of his birth when he returns home after five years in England. But his hatred of India, so clearly voiced in chapter 8 ("he had hated it at first" [*TWSW*, 46]), gradually softens into acceptance. Krishna is more than a minor character, on hand merely to further the plot surrounding Amrita, and Jhabvala gives a whole though admittedly short chapter to Krishna's thoughts just before the close of the novel. Here Krishna's feelings embody the frustrations of people like his parents, those whose dreams of an independent India have little in common with the political reality. As Yasmine Gooneratne explains, "The doubts and ambiguous uncertainties expressed by Krishna in the brief and very important Chapter 37 are repeated, much more powerfully stated yet still unresolved, in Ruth Jhabvala's essay 'Myself in India'" (Gooneratne, 45). In that essay Jhabvala succinctly examines just what attitudes are possible to certain personalities, of certain backgrounds, at certain times, under certain influences. These are questions she raises repeatedly in all her work.

In *To Whom She Will* and *The Nature of Passion* Jhabvala's characters are almost exclusively Indian, and the interest in Western characters in India that marks all her later "Indian" novels has not yet surfaced. Though she is undoubtedly aware of the hardships that must be endured by the great majority in India, she chooses in these novels to express the delight she discovered in her newly adopted country. Both *To Whom She Will* and *The Nature of Passion* must be seen as novels of the first stage of the cycle

Jhabvala believes all Westerners pass through: "tremendous enthusiasm—
everything Indian is marvellous" ("Myself in India," 9).

Yet even in these early novels there is evidence of a repeating, subtly
shifting pattern of interplaying forces, and what Jhabvala does, com-
mendably without restrictive authorial judgments, is to examine all
these kaleidoscopic effects in motion. To stop at a particular judgment,
to remain forever at a particular stage of the cycle she describes in "Myself
in India," would be paralysis and stasis.

Chapter Three
A Changing Climate
The Middle Indian Novels

Like *To Whom She Will* and *The Nature of Passion*, Ruth Prawer Jhabvala's next three novels, *Esmond in India* (1958), *The Householder* (1960), and *Get Ready for Battle* (1962), are set in Delhi, and like those earlier novels, they focus on the lives of one or two families. They return to many of the subjects present in the first two novels—the joint family, arranged marriages and love matches, conflict between children and parents—and they introduce new subjects—*Esmond in India,* for example, represents the first of Jhabvala's detailed studies of Westerners in India. All three include studies of marriage. *Esmond in India* details the unhappy marriage between Esmond and Gulab and its eventual breakup, *The Householder* shows the uneasy marriage of Prem and Indu developing into a strong bond, and *Get Ready for Battle* portrays the already-failed marriage between Gulzari Lal and Sarla Devi.

Memories of Partition are present in both *To Whom She Will* and *The Nature of Passion*, which focus attention on Punjabi refugee families living in Delhi. In *Esmond in India* Jhabvala shifts her attention to one family that has been actively involved in the struggle for independence and another family that has benefited from India's freedom without having made any sacrifices along the way. Within the environs of these two families Jhabvala explores the meaning of freedom in a free India.

The two families are those of Ram Nath and Har Dayal. Ram Nath, along with his sister Uma and her husband, was actively involved in the freedom movement. As Uma recalls, "we have all of us given all we had. But has it not been worth it, for Our Country, for Our Cause; how else would we have achieved Swaraj if we had not been ready to give all we had, even our lives and the lives of our dearest ones . . ."[1] And indeed they, like Nirad Chakravarty of *To Whom She Will*, had given all they had. Ram Nath had given up his career, forfeited his and his wife's property, and been in and out of prison for the sake of the cause he believed in. Now he and his wife, Lakshmi, live in a small tenement flat in a crowded middle-class area of Delhi. Uma and her husband made similar sacrifices: "Gradually, in the years between 1918 and 1947, as Uma and her husband went in and out of jail, forfeited most of their property to the Government, recklessly spent the rest in the course of campaigns and voluntary work, the furnishings of the house had disappeared, the house itself fallen into decay" (*EII*, 51).

In the end Uma's husband had given his life too, dying in prison while on a hunger strike. There is tragic irony in this; as in *To Whom She Will* and *The Nature of Passion*, Jhabvala has focused much attention on food, and Uma is glad to be able to remember her husband not as a dying man but as one who loved life: "She could still see him tearing up an oven-baked chicken with his hands and eating it with super-human relish. It was strange to think of such a man dying after a hunger-strike" (*EII*, 176). As Yasmine Gooneratne points out, "The struggle for freedom is recalled by those of the novel's characters who were actively involved in it, only through intimate, 'domestic' details" (Gooneratne, 89). A historical novelist would be interested in different recollections too, in meetings with Gandhi, as Gooneratne has suggested; nevertheless, through the intimate memories Ram Nath and Uma do have of the struggle for independence, Jhabvala locates her novel in an India that is still adjusting to its newfound freedom 10 years after the event. Recollections of the struggle for independence and of the roles played by various characters in that struggle allow Jhabvala to contrast the altruistic natures of Ram Nath and Uma with the selfishness of a character like Har Dayal. The many references to India's freedom also provide an ironic backdrop to Esmond's struggle to free himself *from* India.

Har Dayal, unlike Ram Nath and Uma, sacrificed nothing in the cause of Swaraj, or self rule. Like Amrita's grandfather in *To Whom She Will*, he never went to prison and never gave up any of his property or wealth. Now, though, he, not Ram Nath, is the one who is benefiting from India's independence, and it appears that his success and position in life have been achieved on the backs of Ram Nath and others like him. Jhabvala makes this trait clear when Har Dayal recites a poem at a party he attends with his daughter Shakuntala. Although the guests at the party are told that Har Dayal will recite a poem "he has translated himself from the Sanskrit" (*EII*, 63), the reader soon learns that "it was not he who had translated [it] (his Sanskrit had never been very good) but Ram Nath" (*EII*, 63). And this perception of Har Dayal achieving success at the expense of men like Ram Nath is reinforced when Lakshmi vents her rage against him: "When we lost everything, he kept everything, he and his wife and his children. My husband had to go to prison, so that Har Dayal afterwards might become an important man—" (*EII*, 110).

As the focus on Ram Nath and Har Dayal suggests, *Esmond in India* is concerned to a large extent with ideals. Esmond, although he gives his name to the title, is by no means the sole protagonist.

Har Dayal is essentially a romantic, and in many ways he is not very patriotic. At times he feels almost ashamed of his Indian upbringing: "Before I went [to England] what a callow youth I was: I had read nothing, I spoke a terrible babu English and wore very tight suits with waists in which anyway I did not feel at all comfortable. At home I had always worn kurta-pyjama or a dhoti and I hated sitting on a chair instead of on the floor or eating with anything but my fingers" (*EII*, 23). While there is an element of conscious humor in this self-portrait, Har Dayal is nevertheless extremely proud of his time in England. In his romantic way he always pictures Ram Nath in his Cambridge days— "indeed the two thoughts, Ram Nath and Cambridge, were for him always intertwined" (*EII*, 23)—despite the fact that such memories bear no resemblance to the Ram Nath we see in the novel. Har Dayal's ideals are as vague as his memories, and change to suit his own self-interest: "Nowadays he liked to think of himself as devoted to the Public Cause; just as before—before '47—he had liked to think of himself as upholding private values in the face of too great a devotion to the Public Cause" (*EII*, 46).

And while Har Dayal likes to think of himself and his daughter Shakuntala as having strong ideals, he is actually quite worried by the thought that Shakuntala might accept the physician Narayan as a husband because of his altruistic dedication to village practice: "Har Dayal's greatest fear . . . was that Shakuntala would be too serious about him. He knew her idealist principles and feared that she might be eager to seize this opportunity of putting them into practice" (*EII*, 123). But Har Dayal need have no fears, for Shakuntala's ideals, like his own, are of a romantic nature, and she is no more likely to give up the comforts she enjoys, her gramophone records, or her outings to the WWO (Western Women's Organization) for the hardships of village life than Har Dayal himself was likely to sacrifice his comforts to join the freedom movement. To admit the shallowness of his daughter's ideals, however, would mean admitting as much about his own, and he has always managed to avoid doing this.

Shakuntala shares the romantic ideals of her father, his love of poetry, art, and music, and his liking for gracious living, but she is a less convincing character. When she dreams of being a famous poet, her thoughts are of Sarojini Naidu: "Perhaps she would be a poet and the revered companion of great men, like Sarojini Naidu. How proud Daddyji would be of her" (*EII*, 12). But it is ironic that Shakuntala should compare herself with Sarojini Naidu, not only a poet but a political freedom fighter, and think how pleased her father would be, for her father has never made any of the sacrifices made by people like Sarojini Naidu and would not wish his daughter to make any either.

Shakuntala's romanticism may be appealing early in the book, and it may complement her father's, but it is exaggerated in her association with Esmond Stillwood. That she throws herself at Esmond and then spends the night with him is surprising, even when her liberal upbringing is taken into account; it is hard to image Amrita or Nimmi behaving in such a manner. Shakuntala's very emancipated behavior does provide a clear contrast to the stubbornly traditional outlook of Gulab, but is it credible that Gulab would have defied the wishes of her family and insisted on marrying Esmond rather than Amrit, when she is afraid of other men even looking at her? Or, as Yasmine Gooneratne asks, is it likely that Madhuri would have allowed the match between Gulab and Amrit to have been arranged in the first place, knowing as we do her hostile attitude toward the families of Ram Nath and Uma (Gooneratne, 113)? Shakuntala's romantic nature prevents her from grasping the fact that Esmond's unhappiness stems not from his marriage to Gulab but from his feeling of entrapment in India itself. Despite her experiences, Shakuntala remains at the end of the novel the spoiled young woman she was at its beginning. It is somewhat surprising that neither Ram Nath nor Uma is able to see through Shakuntala's naive romanticism and professed enthusiasm for ideals similar to their own. But perhaps the very fact that she professes enthusiasm for such ideals explains why they are taken in—after all, Har Dayal too is similarly deceived by his daughter's enthusiasm.

Ram Nath does not share any of Har Dayal's romanticism. He is a man of strong principles who over the years has given up everything for his ideals. Like Har Dayal, Shakuntala, in a romantic way, is aware of this: "Ram Nath Uncle was an Idealist; and even if you were nobody, as he now was, it was always a great thing to be an Idealist. A great and wonderful thing, she thought" (*EII*, 41). Har Dayal often feels guilty about his past, particularly when he is thinking of Ram Nath, but his friend has no such regrets: "He knew that it was pleasant and comfortable to have money, privacy, and privilege: only he had exchanged these things for others which to him personally meant more" (*EII*, 130).

Ram Nath's son, Narayan, has also been willing to give up these comforts for his own values: "He never consulted anyone about what he intended to do, but only announced his decisions when he had made them: 'I shall become a doctor,' had been the first; the second, 'I am joining a Community Health project and shall live and work in small villages in backward areas,'" (*EII*, 50). In doing so he gave up his own comfort and the opportunity of a practice in Delhi that undoubtedly would have made him a rich man. Thus, as Shakuntala resembles her father, so Narayan resembles Ram Nath in his willingness to make sacrifices for his ideals. His idealism, however, is far more convincing than Shankuntala's naive romanticism, perhaps because Jhabvala hints at the misgivings Narayan no doubt suffers about his chosen path. Narayan, not Shakuntala, is able to enjoy freedom in postindependence India because he is prepared to make the sacrifices she will not make.

In *To Whom She Will* Jhabvala made much of the contrasts between Hari's family and Amrita's family, and again in this novel the two families on which she focuses are frequently contrasted. The contrast between Har Dayal and Ram Nath is evident in their respective views of the past:

"I also often think about the past," Har Dayal told Ram Nath in a voice that was almost appealing. "About Cambridge and our youth together and how we read Shakespeare and Shelley and Wordsworth."

"Oh that past," said Ram Nath with a smile. "It is so remote, often I wonder whether it was not in a previous life." (*EII*, 180).

And in one sense it was. For Ram Nath the past is not a romantic memory of Cambridge but the reality of the struggle for independence and the hard times he and others like him had to endure.

Yet although Jhabvala contrasts Har Dayal and Ram Nath, she portrays neither of them as an ideal figure, and indeed both fail to do what is asked of them. Har Dayal, in refusing to agree to the proposed marriage between Shakuntala and Narayan, realizes "how he had just failed Ram Nath and refused him the only thing he had ever asked of him" (*EII*, 180–81), despite his apparent ardent desire to do something for his friend: "Always, when his friend came, his first impulse was to want to fling everything he had at his feet" (*EII*, 68). But Har Dayal is not and never has been true to his ideals. We sympathize with him, however, because he does feel genuine guilt: "he wanted simultaneously to justify himself about the past in which they had gone to jail and he had not, about the present in which he was busy and important and they were not, and about Shakuntala" (*EII*, 182). If Har Dayal's faults are due to his lack of real ideals and his lack of genuine commitment to anything but his own and his family's comfort, Ram Nath's faults can be seen to be caused by the opposite instincts: his too-strong attachment to his ideals, even at the expense of his family's comfort. He finally realizes this failing after Har Dayal's evasive response to the marriage proposal: "instead of expanding and taking in all the world, he had narrowed and could see only himself and his own path. Then he thought that perhaps in many things his wife was right. He laughed at her because she expressed her desire for wealth and position so crudely. But it was not really a desire that could be laughed at, because so many people had it. One had to adjust oneself to all these other people. Now he saw that he had forgotten how to do so" (*EII*, 130).

Lakshmi, Ram Nath's wife, has suffered most from Ram Nath's commitment to his ideals—ideals which she has never shared but for which she has had to make many sacrifices nevertheless. In this and other respects it may be that Ram Nath resembles Gandhi, whose strong devotion to his ideals was perhaps at the expense of his family and in particular his wife, who did not always understand or agree with her husband's actions. Ram Nath's ideals have caused him to be as selfish as Har Dayal—more so in some respects, because he has not even considered the needs of his own family. His refusal to show Lakshmi the letters from their son, Narayan, seems particularly heartless when he knows just how much pleasure he is denying her. He is redeemed somewhat by the very strength of his ideals and because he does realize how Lakshmi has suffered, and he does regret that suffering. Ram Nath also realizes that he has failed his son: "so that now when Narayan—for the first time—called on him to do something for him, he could not do it because he had allowed himself to lose touch" (*EII*, 194). In other words, Ram Nath has allowed his ideals to become a retreat over the years, and in so doing he has lost touch with the reality of everyday life. Indeed, our final view of Ram Nath is one where we see him admitting, to himself at least, his regrets about his withdrawal from life and from others: "He had known all the smells and sounds and sights of the day and the night: and he had always promised himself that one day, when he grew old, he would sit and think about that deep thrill which they gave him and would ferret out their meaning. Well, he had grown old: and up till now he had not even noticed that he had ceased to notice them" (*EII*, 195).

Uma, Ram Nath's sister, shares her brother's ideals and, like Ram Nath, spent considerable time in prison during the struggle for independence. Yet whereas Ram Nath could be described as a modern rationalist, Uma is most definitely a traditionalist, as their differing attitudes toward the need for Gulab to leave her husband illustrate: "For him it was simply, 'Gulab must go away from her husband, today, at once, because he is making her unhappy.' His logical, emancipated mind saw no obstacle. But he knew that for his sister it was different. She was a free, bold, courageous woman; when she thought something was right, she allowed nothing to stand in her way. But the old traditions were in her, and often it took her a long and hard time to overcome them" (*EII*, 28). Because she has maintained these traditional values, Uma has kept in touch with everyday living and understands more clearly than her brother does just how their lives have changed. Uma is the first of Jhabvala's strong women characters. An equally strong and more complex female character is later developed in Sarla Devi of *Get Ready for Battle.*

Although he himself has no ideals, Amrit's comments about his father (Har Dayal) and Ram Nath are not entirely unjust, despite Shakuntala's objections. Referring to his father's committees, he comments that they "are very nice to keep old gentlemen busy but why do we pretend they serve any useful purpose?" (*EII*, 44). Amrit's words firmly place Har Dayal alongside such people as Lady Ram Prashad Khanna and Tarla Mathur of *To Whom She Will* and Mrs. Kaul of *A Backward Place*. On the subject of ideals Amrit adds, "There is Ram Nath Uncle who, so they tell me, is full of ideals. And please just tell me where they have brought him?" (*EII*, 45). While he has no time for ideals, he is nevertheless quite tolerant of those who do. His criticism is offered good-humoredly and should be so taken by Ram Nath. After all, at times Amrit's understanding of others—of his father, his sister, even of Ram Nath himself—is perhaps greater than Ram Nath's own. Unlike Om Prakesh in *The Nature of Passion*, Amrit is quite happy to accept that other people are different; he is secure enough in his own world not to feel threatened by Ram Nath and, unlike his father, feels no guilt about his position.

Neither Lakshmi nor Har Dayal's wife, Madhuri, when the situation arises, has any time for the ideals of her husband. The marriage between Ram Nath and Lakshmi, like the marriage in *To Whom She Will* between Radha and Nirad Chakravarty (who was also involved in the freedom struggle against his wife's wishes), is an example of an arranged marriage that has not worked. Even though Lakshmi does appear to show a genuine affection for her husband on occasions, Ram Nath and Lakshmi have never had anything in common; Lakshmi has steadfastly refused to associate herself with the freedom struggle that has been Ram Nath's life. Only once in the novel does Lakshmi see herself as part of that struggle, and then only because she is so indignant at Har Dayal's refusal to agree to the proposed marriage between Narayan and Shakuntala; she associates herself with Ram Nath and Uma only to dissociate herself from Har Dayal and his family: "'We sacrificed everything in order that Our India might be free—' Uma was so startled that she dropped the thread: Lakshmi had always hitherto so carefully disassociated herself from the Independence struggle" (*EII*, 191). In fact, Lakshmi has always been jealous of Madhuri, who has been able to exert an influence over Har Dayal that she herself has never been able to exert over Ram Nath: "Madhuri had at one time feared that he might follow the general madness and throw himself into the Independence movement. . . . [I]t had only been by exerting all her influence and bringing it to bear on the side of his other predilection for comfortable living that she had managed to counteract it" (*EII*, 168–69).

Neither woman, then, has any time for ideals, and they are in many ways very similar characters; neither woman is a fool, and both understand the comfort of a material outlook on life. Madhuri succeeds where Lakshmi fails only because of her husband's weaker nature. Whereas over the years Har Dayal has submitted to Madhuri's wishes and indeed his own desire for comfort, he has always been patriotic enough to respect Ram Nath's ideals, which Lakshmi, Madhuri, and Amrit fail to do. Despite their many shortcomings, Har Dayal and Shakuntala do at least respect Ram Nath.

All the Indian characters in the novel, though some of them may not have strong ideals in the sense that Ram Nath, Uma, or Narayan may understand them, do at least believe in the ideal of serving those closest to them. Esmond alone exhibits no ideals and accordingly is seen as callous and inconsiderate in comparison to the other characters. Ruth Prawer Jhabvala may not put Ram Nath forward as a model, but she does suggest the importance of having some ideals by presenting Esmond as being at the opposite extreme.

With the character of Esmond, whom Haydn Williams describes as "a minor Lovelace dropped out of Richardson's *Clarissa* (Williams, 29), Jhabvala introduces a darker level into her writing. While *Esmond in*

India is still a comedy, Esmond's vicious nature at times makes it a rather dark one. Esmond's nature—a mixture of romanticism and cynicism—is supported by no ideals at all, not even the ideal of service to those closest to him, which at least Har Dayal has always had. Esmond's marriage is a clear example of this nature: "he had wanted an Indian son, a real piece of India, as he had wanted an Indian wife" (*EII*, 34). The marriage is a failure because neither he nor Gulab put any effort into making it work, and its failure provides the battleground for the first of Jhabvala's many cross-cultural confrontations. Like James and Forster, Jhabvala turns from intersocial confrontations to intercultural ones. And it is possible that conscious parallels exist between *Esmond in India* and *The Portrait of a Lady*. Gilbert Osmond in Henry James's novel is, like Esmond Still-wood, a ghastly, sterile character who marries for aesthetic reasons. The purely aesthetic approach to culture and the desire to possess it are shown by James and Jhabvala to be destructive.

Esmond may understand Indian culture from a distance, as his lectures suggest, but he has no real tolerance or feeling for the Indian way of life, as shown in his refusal to allow Ravi to have his head shaved—a symbolic ceremony that Esmond now chooses to label a barbaric custom—or in his insistence that only English food be served in his home. Here Jhabvala turns once again to food to draw contrasts between two characters, Gulab loves to eat the hot spicy food sent from her mother's house: "She sat on the floor and ate with her fingers. She always did so, whenever Esmond was out, for that was the way she enjoyed her food most" (*EII*, 17). When Esmond returns home for his lunch soon afterward, it is a very different scene: "He sat alone at his smart little dining-table in his smart little dining-corner and ate his cheese salad. Everything on the table was colourful and modern—the bright table-mats, the painted drinking-glass, the earthenware plates of a rich dark green—so that it looked rather like a beautifully photographed full-page advertisement in an American magazine. It was very different from Gulab's spicy meal eaten on the floor out of brass bowls" (*EII*, 32–33). This passage recalls the contrast Jhabvala drew between the meals at the Rai Bahadur's and at Hari's house in *To Whom She Will*.

Esmond is the first major European character in Jhabvala's novels. Like so many of her European characters, Esmond feels himself trapped in and overwhelmed by India: "He decided to go and see Betty. He always, whenever he felt particularly oppressed by Gulab, went to see Betty. Her flat was so light, modern, and airy; she herself so light, modern, and airy. Being with her was almost as good as being in

England—which was the one place where he wanted most passionately to be" (*EII*, 39). Like Professor Hoch before him, Esmond sees himself as an expert on Indian culture. But again like Professor Hoch, Esmond is seen differently by some of the Indians with whom he comes into contact: "The servant wondered what the Sahib was saying; he could not even identify the language he was talking. Esmond, who rather enjoyed listening to himself speaking in Hindustani, gave him a long and sonorous lecture on his duties" (*EII*, 33). This subtle deflating of Esmond continues when Jhabvala presents Esmond's linguistic abilities through Western rather than Indian eyes: "of course, he had been in India a long time and had an Indian wife and spoke such fluent Hindustani. He could really talk to these people like one of themselves" (*EII*, 61). This admiration for Esmond's accomplishments voiced by a Western lady is not, however, shared by her male compatriots, who see Esmond as a joke rather than an expert on Indian culture, as the heavy irony in the following piece of dialogue shows:

Shakuntala looked gravely from one to the other and said, "Yes, I have heard he is clever."
"*Tre*-mendously," said the second Englishman, casting his eyes up to the ceiling.
"Didn't you know," said the big red Englishman, "he's come specially to India to teach you people all about your own country." (*EII*, 65)

And Esmond's deflation is complete when, after the "monumental tragedy" of the loss of his shoes from the steps of the Taj Mahal (*EII*, 137), Jhabvala places Esmond in front of the crowd like an Aunt Sally to have him knocked over by Betty, his English friend and lover, who laughs at the ridiculous figure standing before the magnificent monument. And as Meena Belliappa notes, this incident "reveals how out of sympathy he is with the country on which he has amassed so much information."[2] We eventually see that Esmond's true idea of Indian culture is to sit drinking tea and making polite conversation in Madhuri's drawing room. But this is hardly the real India, and because he realizes this Esmond longs to return to England. Only Betty fully understands his disillusion and is capable of seeing his selfish nature.

Through Esmond Jhabvala traces for the first time in her fiction the cycle, described in "Myself in India," she believes all Westerners in India must go through. Esmond had clearly been at the first stage of the cycle—"everything Indian is marvellous"—when he married Gulab.

During the five years between his marriage and the period of the novel, he has passed through the second stage—"everything Indian not so marvellous"—and has entered the final stage—"everything Indian abominable." During the course of the novel we see how this stage rapidly overwhelms him and leads him to his decision to leave India forever. All this is reflected in his relationship with Gulab, who for Esmond represents his India.

Esmond reacts, finally, against everything he sees around him, the poverty, the dirt, the heat, all symbolized, for the first time in Jhabvala's fiction, by "the Indian sky—an unchanging, unending expanse of white-blue glare, the epitome of meaningless monotony which dwarfed all human life into insignificance" (*EII*, 202). Instead he runs to the relative comfort of England, "where there were solid grey houses and solid grey people, and the sky was kept within decent proportions" (*EII*, 202). Although the link between her own feelings toward India, as explained in "Myself in India," and Esmond's feelings is not fully made in this novel, seven years later, in *A Backward Place*, Jhabvala does explore her own feelings in far greater detail through the characters of Etta (who resembles Esmond in certain respects) and Judy.

In *Esmond in India* Ruth Prawer Jhabvala makes her first reference to E. M. Forster's monumental novel *A Passage to India*, a book Jhabvala would later feel she had to confront, to write back to, an influence she had to exorcise in her fiction. Here, though, there is just one passing reference to Forster's novel, made by Esmond as he travels to Agra with the WWO excursion: "'And on your right,' declaimed Esmond, 'you will see the historic spot where Mr. E. M. Forster first met Miss Adela Quested while she sat taking notes for her Social Science class'" (*EII*, 119). This fleeting reference is an acknowledgment that Jhabvala assumes all her readers will have read Forster's novel, just as Esmond assumes all his listeners are familiar with it.

Esmond in India also looks ahead to Jhabvala's later novels in its description, permitted by the excursion to Agra, of the Indian landscape: "It was dull. There was only the road, running through the dry, barren, anonymous landscape. When they came to a village, it was always the same village, as dry and dusty as the surrounding landscape. . . . The sun became hotter every minute, making of sky and earth one vast white bowl of dust" (*EII*, 116). This stark description stands in marked contrast to the picture Jhabvala presents of the crowded streets around Ram Nath's home, a picture that recalls similar scenes around Hari Sahni's house in *To Whom She Will*. For the first time Jhabvala's characters move beyond the vicinity of "home," and thus a wider picture of India is offered than the essentially domestic one she presents in the first two novels and returns to in *The Householder*. Like Jhabvala's first two novels, *Esmond in India* is a novel of contrasts, and while her delight in India is no longer unfettered, it is by no means extinguished.

The question of arranged marriages and love matches, though not of the same importance in this novel as in the earlier ones, is still apparent. Amrit's marriage to Indira was arranged by their families and is seen to be a happy bond. Although we may agree with Ram Nath that Amrit is a "complete fool" (*EII*, 79), we can also see that Indira appears to be happy with him, just as Gulab no doubt would have been had she not refused him in favor of Esmond. As in the cases of Amrita's and Nimmi's arranged marriages, there is a suggestion that Indira "had begun to care for Amrit even before her parents had directed her to do so" (*EII*, 126). In *Esmond in India* it is not always the older generation who initiate arranged marriages; Narayan writes to his father appealing to Ram Nath to find him a wife. And the theme of arranged marriage versus love match is further extended in this novel by using it to introduce, again for the first time in Jhabvala's novels, the conflict between East and West. Shakuntala is full of admiration, even envy, for Gulab, "because Gulab had been so brave and had refused to let herself be satisfied with the ordinary" (*EII*, 12). Yet ironically Gulab desires nothing that is extraordinary. Thus, like Lalaji and his wife in *The Nature of Passion*, Gulab is not at ease in her well-furnished flat: "Gulab could not see any purpose for so much furniture; it only prevented one from being comfortable" (*EII*, 16). And she is even less comfortable with Esmond's attempts to fit her into his Western idea of a wife: "She was still in the sari which she wore at night; it was crumpled and torn, but she felt at ease in it. It had been different when Esmond had made her wear those flimsy transparent nightdresses with lace and ruffles and ribbons; then she had put on her clothes the moment she had got out of bed for she had felt so indecent" (*EII*, 16). Esmond has never really been in love with Gulab or with India, only with Gulab's beauty and with the aesthetic charm of India. Jhabvala uses Gulab's marriage to Esmond to present the clashes between traditional and modern values in a more complex way than in her previous novels—partly because for the first time she presents the consequences of arranged marriage and introduces the added interest of a cross-cultural marriage, and partly because Gulab, despite her marriage, is no rebel: the traditional values, previously embodied in older family members, are shown to be strong in Gulab.

These strong traditional values make Gulab refuse even to consider leaving her husband, despite her mother's earnest entreaties and despite her knowledge of his infidelities. Only when she is attacked by their servant does Gulab leave Esmond, and she does so at that juncture without hesitation. We as readers have been aware of the servant watching Gulab and have seen the warnings of the threat to her. By showing us these signs Jhabvala is suggesting that Esmond too should have been able to see them, had he cared enough.

The note of discord struck in *Esmond in India* is forgotten temporarily in *The Householder*, which sees what Laurie Sucher has aptly described as "a return to the harmonious vision of the first two novels, in a more melancholy, almost elegiac, mode."[3]

Whereas *To Whom She Will* and *The Nature of Passion* describe the events and misunderstandings that finally lead to the prospects of happy marriage, *The Householder* is primarily a study of an arranged marriage that has already taken place. The central figure of the novel, Prem, a Hindi teacher in a private college, is newly married and has only recently arrived in Delhi. The novel sees him embark on the second stage of a traditional Hindu life, that of the householder. As Prem explains (for the benefit of the reader) to Mr. Seigal, his landlord:

"there are four stages to a man's life. When he is young, he is a student, learning from his father and his teachers. . . .

"After that comes the life of the householder," Prem said, "In this stage a man must raise a family and see to their needs. . . . The third stage is when a man retires from his duties as a householder and spends his time in contemplation."[4]

The fourth stage, which Prem cannot remember, is when a man renounces the world and takes up the life of a sannyasi.

The Householder is at the same time Jhabvala's most comic and most tender novel. Much of the comedy comes from Prem's naive view of himself and from his immaturity, both of which are cleverly exposed by Jhabvala. He takes his position as husband, householder, and teacher very seriously, as Jhabvala shows in the novel's opening lines:

Prem sat at the only table they had and corrected his students' essay papers. The table was a very frail and shaky one, made of thin cane, and it would have been more comfortable to sit on the floor. But he felt there was a certain dignity about sitting at a table; his father had always sat at a table when correcting papers. It was unreasonable, of course, to consider dignity, when there was no chance of any of his students seeing him; but he considered he would feel better for it afterwards, when he was returning their papers. He was not too good at enforcing discipline, and that made him a little afraid of his students and in need of all the moral support he could give himself. (*TH*, 7).

This passage illustrates Jhabvala's methods in the book as a whole. In the opening sentence Prem's position as a teacher is clearly stated, only to be undermined by the "frail and shaky" table he works at, suggesting the equally frail and shaky hold he has on the absurd dignity he attaches to his job. That Prem sees his dignity reinforced by his position at this inadequate table shows the reader how seriously he takes his own role, yet in the following sentences Jhabvala undermines Prem's attitude to his work by showing also how precariously balanced Prem is in the position, and by showing that while he may take himself seriously as a teacher, it appears that few others do. And what applies to his position as a teacher applies equally to his position as husband and father-to-be and as a householder, as the pages that follow illustrate. But Prem is not simply or harshly deflated by the author; his lack of confidence is at all times tenderly portrayed.

Prem's dissatisfaction with his marriage and with his wife, Indu—dissatisfaction stemming largely from his naïveté about marriage—and his concern about his small salary and large rent combine to make him genuinely unhappy and also lonely. He longs to talk to someone, to share and discuss his problems, but ironically he doesn't turn to Indu, who is equally lonely and unhappy, though the thought does cross his mind: "He very much needed someone to laugh with and to talk to and confide in. How wonderful if it could have been Indu, with whom he lived and who lay beside him at night" (*TH*, 34). But Prem, instead of trying to break down the barrier between them, speaks harshly to Indu, in an attempt to assert himself as a husband in a way that is both comic in its absurdity and tragic in its innocent immaturity. After an unusually heated argument, Prem forces himself to buy Indu a present of sweet-meats, a gesture that unlocks a door between them and heralds a new stage in the development of their relationship, as well as of Prem's understanding of Indu and thus of his role as husband. In this moment of happiness they can make love without embarrassment, despite its being daytime, a contrast to the guilty feeling Prem earlier experienced whenever he felt desire for Indu. Sadly, though, the inopportune arrival of Prem's mother prevents their relationship from progressing any further at this stage.

The arrival of Prem's mother draws attention to one of the major obstacles standing in the way of Prem and Indu's relationship, namely his habit of comparing his own situation with an idealized picture of his parents' marriage, in which, "[a]s far as he was aware, his mother had not been in the habit of defying his father" (*TH*, 28). Thus he sees Indu's insistence on returning to her parents as a sign of his own failure as a husband. Prem sees in his father a successful man whom he must strive to live up to, not least in terms of discipline both at home and at school; he also sees in his father the security of his student days, free from the worries and responsibilities he now has to face—a reflection of his continuing immaturity.

Because of this desire to return to the security of his student days, Prem clings to his old friend Raj, who now also lives in Delhi. But Raj, a government officer with a young child to support, has no time to consider Prem's problems or to look back fondly on their early life in Ankhpur: "The only two things Raj seemed to be interested in now were his job and his family" (*TH*, 16), the two things Prem is having difficulty coming to terms with. Though he appears to want to forget his present problems and talk only about their college days when he is with Raj, Prem does in fact want to talk about his family and his job. Raj is one of the people Prem turns to for guidance, seeing him as already established in the householder stage of life, and his failure to broach his problems in Raj's company further adds to his sense of failure. When Prem visits his friend at home, after Raj has twice failed to turn up for their previously regular Monday meetings, he finally realizes that Raj is no longer the youth he knew but instead a husband and father with many responsibilities and worries of his own: "Prem looked at him with respect. He felt there was much he could learn from Raj" (*TH*, 69). Similarly, when he visits Raj at his office Prem realizes he is not alone in having to contend with problems at work. His reasons for wanting a government job show his increasing through still naive sense of responsibility: "But he found it difficult to explain what this was. The fact that he wanted to belong somewhere; and not only that, but also his whole position as householder, as husband, which he wanted to stabilize, register as it were, make sure and accepted. He was so different from the Prem who had been a student in Ankhpur College and had lived in his father's house" (*TH*, 101). Although he cannot put these feelings into words, he does effectively show the change in himself when he telephones Raj to formally invite him round for a meal: "Now, when he and Indu had cooked for and entertained their own guests, they would have grown to their full stature of householders and married couple" (*TH*, 129), which proves to be the case.

Prem is not so successful in his attempts to raise his salary and lower his rent. Neither of his attempts to ask for a higher salary do anything other than irritate the principal's wife, Mrs. Khanna, and he becomes very concerned about his failings at the school. He compares himself with his colleague Mr. Chaddha (in much the same way as he compares himself with the memory of his father) and is "[i]rritated by [the] contrast between his own and Mr. Chaddha's students" (*TH*, 10). Though Prem clearly dislikes Mr. Chaddha, he nevertheless looks up to him and admires his confidence, as his thoughts following the principal's college tea party show: "How he wished then that he had had the courage to get up and make a speech, like Mr. Chaddha!" (*TH*, 76). Next to this man Prem feels his own failings as a teacher all the more sharply, just as next to his father he keenly felt his failings as a husband.

At various times in the novel Prem looks up to Mr. Khanna, Mr. Chaddha, and Raj, hoping one of them will recognize in him a young man who is entering the householder stage and is in need of advice and encouragement. Because none of these persons appear to take Prem seriously as a teacher or as a husband and householder, he turns elsewhere for guidance. And, true to his character, Prem turns in the wrong direction, to his shy colleague Sohan Lal, whose failings are as obvious as his own: "He realized that he should be looking up to Mr. Chaddha and trying to emulate him; and he wondered why it was that he should feel more drawn towards Sohan Lal, who was manifestly unsuccessful and unconfident" (*TH*, 37). (Sohan Lal is the only true figure of pathos in the novel, and as Yasmine Gooneratne rightly indicates, he "is the only character in *The Householder* who is not a source of comedy" [Gooneratne, 117].) As Sohan Lal's failings are so obvious, Prem finds himself able to talk to him in the way he had hoped to be able to talk to Raj. Although he likes Sohan Lal, Prem is fully aware of his shortcomings as a teacher; after Mr. Chaddha's rebuke in the classroom, which humiliates him in front of his students, followed by the threat of dismissal from Mr. Khanna, Prem finally faces up to the fact that his position is no different from that of Sohan Lal or thousands like him: "He was on one side with Indu behind him and the coming baby, and on the other side were the Khannas and the Seigals and Mr. Chaddha and his students and doctor's bills and income tax forms and all the other horrors the world had in store for him. He felt that he was required to pit his strength against all these, and yet he knew from the beginning that it was hopeless because he did not have much strength. He knew that the only way he could survive was by submitting to and propitiating the other side" (*TH*, 125).

In the end Prem becomes resigned to his position, and his dissatisfaction turns inevitably to acceptance. He has been unsuccessful in his attempts to have his salary raised and his rent lowered, but because he is now secure in his position as a husband and a householder, he will no doubt be able to cope with these other problems. The novel ends on a high note, with the success of the meal Indu has prepared for Raj and his wife, and with it Raj's acceptance of Prem as a husband and householder. But this happiness is tinged by the reader's knowledge that life will continue to be a struggle for Prem. He will no doubt adopt Sohan Lal's attitude at work, and when Prem and Indu attend the wedding of Sohan Lal's relative in Mehrauli, there is also the shadow of a suggestion that Prem will become like Sohan Lal in other ways too: "'It is nice here,' . . . 'And rents are cheap,' he said. But he knew that he did not want to come and live here. . . . [H]e was too proud of having established himself in a big town like Delhi" (*TH*, 131). With his low salary and high rent, Prem may eventually have no alternative but to move to a place like Mehrauli.

Through his friendship with Sohan Lal Prem meets the swami, the first of numerous swamis and gurus to appear in Jhabvala's novels. Unlike many of his ilk who appear in the later novels, this swami is essentially a positive figure, one whose words give Prem confidence, even if that confidence does not last long. His words, unlike the words of many of his successors, are not empty; his parables have meaning and relate to the central concerns of the novel. The parable he relates on Prem's first visit suggests that Prem, who is in many ways superior to the likes of Mr. Khanna or Mr. Siegal, is not aware of his true worth and, further, that his worth is overlooked by others (Gooneratne,131). But Prem is not free to devote his life to the swami; he has material responsibilities that must take precedence over his spiritual desires. Prem realizes this when he turns, somewhat sadly, away from the swami. Before he can consider a spiritual life, which comes in the third and fourth stages of Hindu life, he must first consolidate his position in the second stage, as a householder.

The European characters in this novel are quite different from those in *Esmond in India*. Prem's association with Hans Loewe and Kitty is comically portrayed, as this piece of dialogue between Kitty and Prem illustrates:

"What do you do?"

"I am a lecturer at—"

"No, dear. Which Yoga do you do? Hatha Yoga or Bhakti Yoga or what?"

"I don't think I—"

"Well you should." (*TH*, 43)

Through Prem's acquaintance with Kitty, and the party he attends with her and Hans, Jhabvala is able to show not only an Indian view of Europeans—"Their interest in spiritual matters puzzled him, for he had always thought that Europeans were very materialistic in their outlook" (*TH*, 46)—but also European views of Indians: "They all look spiritual" (*TH*, 44). Kitty's apparently simple remark can actually be read in two very different ways. With the stress on *all* ("They *all* look spiritual"), it suggests the difficulties Kitty is experiencing in her own spiritual quest while everyone around her seems to be succeeding. But with the stress on *look* ("They all *look* spiritual"), the meaning would then be that Indians may look spiritual but in fact are not—which is what the woman with the bead necklace appears to be suggesting at the party (*TH*, 64). Hans himself is frequently a figure of amusement, both in his appearance and in his philosophizing about Indian spirituality, philosophizing Prem is never able to understand. Although Hans is only a minor figure who adds to the comedy of the novel, his decision to leave Delhi in search of a guru does look ahead to the European seekers of the later novels, *A New Dominion* and *Heat and Dust*, and such stories as "A Spiritual Call" and "How I Became a Holy Mother."

A tender comedy also surrounds Prem's relationship with Indu, based on their shyness with and misunderstanding of each other. Prem hurriedly eats a bag of nuts before he returns home because he doesn't know how to offer Indu some, and his embarrassment over Indu's pregnancy is both delightfully comic and touching: "Her pregnancy was a terrible embarrassment for him. Now everybody would know what he did with her at night in the dark" (*TH*, 8).

Indeed, the major source of comedy in *The Householder* seems to be caused by Prem's embarrassment, which frequently stems from his own immaturity. This embarrassment is often seen in Prem's contact with those people who have some control over his life and whom he thinks should be sympathetic toward him. The scene of his greatest discomfort, the college tea party, where Indu "was continually biting, chewing, licking her fingers or flicking crumbs from her lips with her tongue" (*TH*, 74) against the background of Mr. Chaddha's pompous speech and

Mrs. Khanna's obvious disapproval, is one of the most amusing passages in the whole of Jhabvala's writing.

Although he had initially thought he should strive to be like Mr. Khanna or Mr. Chaddha, Prem does come to realize that he doesn't want to be like either of them, and this realization is a further step on his path to maturity. Similarly, while he may desire the comfort his landlords, the Seigals, enjoy, there is a touch of comedy in his disapproval of their way of life: "Somehow he could not help feeling a tinge of disapproval at their nightly card-parties, the lights and the noise and the radio, the whisky, the cups of tea and the plates of sweetmeats so freely circulated. He did not think that such ease was conducive to a really noble life" (*TH*, 20).

But the real steps on Prem's path to maturation take place at home, in his relationship with Indu. When Indu leaves without a word, he is forced into the realization that he loves her: "For the first time he thought about how he felt about her: yes, he thought, he had begun to grow fond of her" (*TH*, 85). In an indirect way he states his love in the material he buys for her but never gives her and in the letter he writes but doesn't post. And when she returns, Indu admits her love for Prem, even though she cannot bring herself to tell him, except in a roundabout way: "Yes, now you have important letters to post! But when I am away, not one line could you write to me, though I waited and waited" (*TH*, 108). The irony in the reference to the letter Prem has posted is significant and doubled-edged: the reference not only is to the letter Prem has just posted to his sister in Bangalore, which will free Prem and Indu from the burden of his mother, but also recalls the honest letter, full of feeling, that Prem never did post. His prompt decision to bundle his mother off to Bangalore is another important step toward a maturity that is perhaps realized when, despite the new threat of possible dismissal hanging over him, he is able to turn away from the security of the past: "He even began to think rather longingly of his boyhood again: of living in his father's house, looked after by his mother and with no responsibilities except those of passing in his examinations. Yet he knew he did not want that at all. He wanted to be looked after not by his mother but by Indu. And he wanted to look after her" (*TH*, 125). The letter he writes to his sister in Bangalore is probably the most decisive step he takes in the course of the novel. With this letter he symbolically frees himself of his parents' shadow and makes a conscious decision to accept his responsibilities as a husband. Prem's acceptance of Indu, and the couple's happiness, is clearly shown in their unreserved lovemaking the night Prem's mother leaves, a scene beautifully described by Jhabvala.

Consequently, Prem's unsuccessful attempt to have his rent lowered results not in more despondency or a renewed longing for his childhood but in the mature realization "that no one was interested in his difficulties, that the problem of supporting himself and Indu and any family they might have was his alone" (*TH*, 126). And with the process of maturation complete, Prem is able to look at the "glum bridegroom" and smile "with superior knowledge" (*TH*, 133) when he attends the wedding in Mehrauli. He can now see himself as an adult of the same stature as his friend Raj. Despite their apparently limited prospects, Prem and Indu in their own way have achieved a freedom that characters like Shakuntala, with all her wealth and comforts, will never experience.

In *Get Ready for Battle* Ruth Prawer Jhabvala once again presents a study in contrasts. The rather-too-unworldly Sarla Devi is contrasted with the very practical and very worldly-wise Kusum, and the ruthless businessman Gulzari Lal—who in many ways is a darker portrait than either of his predecessors, Lalaji of *The Nature of Passion* and Har Dayal of *Esmond in India*—is contrasted with his son Vishnu, who wants to be independent of his father but doesn't know how to achieve his desire. The novel also, as Yasmine Gooneratne notes, contrasts "the luxurious world inhabited by a wealthy businessman with that other world of sickness and destitution which his wife Sarla Devi, a woman of conscience, struggles to alleviate" (Gooneratne, 140).

As the title suggests, the central concern of *Get Ready for Battle* is with battle—that is, with action and duty. The epigraph comes once more from the *Bhagavad Gita*:

Treating alike pleasure and pain, gain and loss, victory and defeat, then get ready for battle.

This is the advice Krishna gives to Arjuna on the battlefield of Kurukshetra, when Arjuna refuses to start the fight that will result in the death of so many of his kinsmen who are lined up against him. Krishna reminds Arjuna of his dharma, which loosely translates as duty, and tells him that as an active man he has only two choices open to him: renunciation or the yoga of action (karma yoga), which requires him to fight.

The many struggles of the novel are intricately woven together and almost inevitably focus on Sarla Devi. Because every conflict in some way includes her, she becomes the central figure, and the reader's attention is directed to Bundi Busti, the slum colony scheduled to be cleared, which thus becomes the major battleground, against which we see all the other struggles and against which all the other battles are placed in their true perspective. Every major character appears to be ready for battle—Kusum, Gulzari Lal, Brij Mohan, Vishnu, even Mala—but Sarla Devi's cause alone is altruistic and not fought for selfish reasons.

Kusum's battle to persuade Gulzari Lal to seek a divorce, despite the fact that she has apparently quite happily been his mistress for the preceding eight years, is obviously selfish. To further her aims she draws his son and daughter-in-law, Vishnu and Mala, into her plans: "She wanted to bring Gulzari Lal to a certain point and saw that she could not do so without some degree of coercion. She made an attempt to explain herself to Mala and to Vishnu, both of whom she needed on her side."[5] Kusum's is a scheming sort of battle: she deliberately quarrels with Gulzari Lal to force him to go and see his wife; she blatantly sets about flattering Sarla Devi's brother, Brij Mohan, in an attempt to overcome his objections to the divorce; and as Ramlal Agarwal suggests, she "feigns love for Vishnu and Mala."[6] As Jhabvala makes clear, Kusum, unlike Sarla Devi, knows how to get around people. She even takes up Sarla Devi's battle for Bundi Busti, though it is contrary to her own ideas, because she considers doing so a necessary part of her battle for the divorce which she thinks Sarla Devi might otherwise refuse to agree to—though in this instance she fails to appreciate Sarla Devi's unselfish nature. Ironically, Kusum expects everyone to act out of selfish motivation, as she herself does. Her scheming does, however, win over Brij Mohan, whom she flatters and bribes out of his objections. Indeed, her whole campaign against Gulzari Lal is successful. Once the divorce is ensured and her place as Gulzari Lal's wife and mistress of his house certain, she can afford to get rid of Vishnu and Mala, which she does by pleading with Gulzari Lal to allow them to go to Chandnipat to live. She may do this at Mala's request, but had it not been to her advantage, she would not have taken up their cause.

Brij Mohan's refusal to agree to his sister's divorce, supposedly to uphold his family's honor, is, of course, in direct opposition to Kusum's major battle. But like Kusum, Brij Mohan acts out of selfish interest, and his opposition is overcome by the promise of future comfort for himself. Brij Mohan's battle is essentially futile; he cannot prevent Sarla Devi from agreeing to the divorce, and his own propensity for drinking and for entertaining whores in his grubby, run-down house has already damaged the family honor more than his sister is likely to do. His battle for compensation for the land and properties he lost during Partition is equally futile and acts as a mirror through which to see his present battle.

Ironically, he sees himself as "The old warrior march[ing] into battle" (*GRB*, 158) as he sets out to visit Kusum, who has already engaged and defeated him.

Vishnu's battle is for independence and is fought against Gulzari Lal (which in some respects is also true of Kusum's and Brij Mohan's battles, and even of Sarla Devi's battle for Bundi Busti). Mala's battle is essentially the same: to stay with Vishnu and to get him away from his father, and in so doing to force him to accept his responsibilities as a married man. (Similar problems face Prem and Indu in *The Householder*; in both cases the marriages are arranged.) Vishnu's main problem is motivation, and only after he has read the excerpt from the *Gita*, "*then get ready for battle*" (*GRB*, 106), over and over again and heard his mother's imploring words, "Do anything you like, son. Only do it" (*GRB*, 106), which recall Krishna urging Arjuna to action, does he have the courage to pursue his interest in Joginder Nath's scheme to manufacture fountain pens, and to ask his father for the necessary capital. All the major characters of the novel are involved in battles of one sort or another, but it is to Vishnu more than anyone else that the words of the title apply, albeit somewhat ironically—the words of the *Gita* encourage one to serve the world disinterestedly, not to act for oneself. He is the one who must be motivated to action, and fittingly the final motivation comes from his mother, Sarla Devi, who more than any other character follows the true philosophy of the *Gita*.

Ironically, Mala rather selfishly sees Chandnipat as a means of bringing her and Vishnu closer together and thinks "only of how completely she would possess him there" (*GRB*, 135), while Vishnu thinks Mala and their daughter, Pritti, could remain in Delhi, where he would visit them "several times a month, or whenever he found the time. Though of course—he thought with satisfaction of those powerful days ahead— there would not be much time" (*GRB*, 143). But this battle is not over until Vishnu finally agrees to take Mala and Pritti with him. In agreeing to take them however, Vishnu has not lost his battle, because "as soon as he had said it he found himself, to his surprise, not altogether displeased" (*GRB*, 158). Rather, he and Mala have won their joint battle for independence, which was their main objective, and perhaps they now realize that they both wanted the same thing, a discovery that could only come about when their selfish secondary motives had been superseded.[7] Vishnu is only just coming to terms with himself, and he, like Prem in *The Householder*, must come to terms with his many conflicting emotions. He is troubled by his father's passion for property and cannot share it, but he cannot share his mother's social conscience either, though he alone of all the characters in the novel genuinely loves Sarla Devi and enjoys spending time with her—a factor that raises him considerably in the reader's estimation. We are also impressed by Vishnu's interest, albeit short-lived, in Guatam's proposal for a school. While he doesn't finally support Guatam, whose moral example would be almost as difficult to live up to as his mother's (even though he does in some respects resemble such woolly idealists as Viddi's coffeehouse friends), Vishnu's decision to go into business is a definite step away from his father's influence, and one achieved by his own will. If Vishnu is not more altruistic, then at least some of the blame must lie at Sarla Devi's feet. While she criticizes his materialism, she has failed him by not having been around to offer an alternative guiding hand to the capitalist pointing finger of Gulzari Lal.

Gulzari Lal is described by Guatam (who shares Sarla Devi's altruism) as "the worst type of man, attached to money and money-making and existing not as a man but only through the things he possesses, like his car, his house, his mistress" (*GRB*, 17). As an independent youth Gulzari Lal had always been ready for battle; now his battle is quite simply to increase his properties and to develop his land regardless of opposition, which, like Lalaji, he knows how to deal with. His interest in the land adjacent to Bundi Busti once again brings Gulzari Lal into direct conflict with Sarla Devi, and despite his decision to buy the land he is troubled by his wife's interest. Vishnu also feels rather guilty about his father's decision, and this concern proves to be one of the factors that bring about his decision to go into business with Joginder Nath. Gulzari Lal is able to overcome any opposition to his development for a price, and Sarla Devi, the only person he cannot buy, is defeated when the inhabitants of Bundi Busti, successfully bribed by Rattan Singh, are no longer prepared to fight. Sarla Devi needs no encouragement to fight, and she stands in stark contrast to the seemingly lazy Vishnu, the rather indolent Mala, and even Gulzari Lal, Kusum, and Brij Mohan, who fight only for selfish reasons and who, when personal gain has been achieved, are quickly ready to lay down their arms. Sarla Devi, on the other hand, never stops fighting, but moves from one battle to the next, spurred on by an unrelenting social conscience, although she does hope that one day she will not have to engage in continuous battle. Thus at the close of the novel Sarla Devi is searching Delhi's red-light district for Tara, the prostitute recently discarded by Brij Mohan, with some vague notion of either rescuing or helping her.

Sarla Devi's battle holds center stage because every other battle is in some way affected by Sarla Devi herself or by Bundi Busti. The essential difference between the battle for Bundi Busti and the other battles is that Sarla Devi is not acting out of selfishness but instead is fighting for a genuine cause. Nevertheless, Jhabvala does not simply put her forward as an ideal, though to Guatam, whose views we come to trust, she is "the ideal of all women" (*GRB*, 17). Mala, on the other hand, suggests early in the book that Sarla Devi "has never cared for anyone, only herself" (*GRB*, 12). At times Sarla Devi's own words appear to support Mala's view: "I am grateful that I am alone at last and can live the way I like" (*GRB*, 38).

The inhabitants of Bundi Busti are both Sarla Devi's cause and her allies. Their readiness for battle is shown in the speeches of their leader, Ramchander, and even in the old woman who sits contentedly squashing lice in the young child's hair. Sarla Devi believes she is fighting for what the slum dwellers themselves want, which distinguishes her fight from that of Mrs. Bhatnagar and her devoted accomplice, Mrs. Dass, who, though ostensibly fighting for the people of Bundi Busti, are in fact working in direct opposition to their wishes.

Mrs. Bhatnagar is one in a long line of committee ladies (which goes back to Lady Ram Prashad Khanna in *To Whom She Will*) satirized by Ruth Prawer Jhabvala in a way that recalls the Charles Dickens of *Bleak House*: "she was much respected for the wide variety of social work in which she was engaged. She was President of the All-India Society for Bringing Hygiene to the Depressed Classes, Vice-President of the All-India Care for Widows Association, Secretary of the All-India Rehabilitation Centre for Immoral Women and Treasurer of the All-India Home-Crafts for Industrial Workers Society" (*GRB*, 96). Unfortunately, as Jhabvala comically demonstrates on a number of occasions, Mrs. Bhatnagar's understanding of her causes does not go beyond these committees. Her attitude toward the people she is supposedly eager to help is disgustingly condescending:

"A very fine plot has been earmarked for them beyond Shahdara," Mrs. Bhatnagar said.

"A beautiful airy place," Mrs. Dass corroborated.

"But they don't want to go," Sarla Devi said in a tone which, if Mrs. Bhatnagar had known her better, would have put her on her guard.

But Mrs. Bhatnagar only smiled in a tolerant manner. "It often happens that children don't know when something is done for their good. We must regard them like children."

"Like children thay must be guided by their elders and betters," Mrs. Dass said, smiling likewise.

But Sarla Devi did not smile at all. "Elders and betters?" she inquired like thunder. (*GRB*, 117)

In her desire to move the people of Bundi Busti, Mrs. Bhatnagar fails to consider the impracticalities, except as they concern her fellow social workers, who, she explains, will be transported to the new site by jeep. Sarla Devi's question, "And are you also providing jeeps to take the inhabitants of Bundi Busti to their work in the city?" (*GRB*, 117), does not interest her; it simply allows her to form a negative picture of Sarla Devi, whom she classes as unpractical.

All Sarla Devi's efforts come to an abrupt end when Ramchander, who has been successfully bribed, is no longer willing to support her. She knows that if she is not fighting for the wishes of the people concerned, then there is no cause, and also that when she is faced with the power of money, she cannot hope to win. Sarla Devi may not have a passion for wealth herself, but she does understand the lure of money, particularly to the poor: "Whatever sum it was they had offered [Ramchander], it had been a fortune for him; and he was in no position to resist a fortune" (*GRB*, 149).

This, the worthiest struggle in the book, ironically ends in failure, and the help offered by Mrs. Bhatnagar is of more use after all. That Sarla Devi, the book's most admirable character, is also ineffective provides a marked and ironic contrast to Kusum's total success. Sadly, there is no place for people like Sarla Devi and Ram Nath of *Esmond in India* in Jhabvala's modern India. That her view of India can no longer accommodate such individuals signals that Jhabvala herself had perhaps reached the end of the second stage of the cycle she describes in "Myself in India"—"everything Indian not so marvellous"—and with *Get Ready for Battle* had entered the third stage—"everything Indian abominable".

Get Ready for Battle in particular shows a departure from the comedy of the first two novels and paints a darker picture of India than *Esmond in India*, which despite its interest in ideals is essentially a comic novel. Harmless characters like Lady Ram Prashad Khanna and Har Dayal, who devote their time to an endless string of committees, are left behind, and in their place Jhabvala has introduced the abominable Mrs. Bhatnagar, whose attitude toward the poor is too despicable to be amusing. *Get Ready for Battle* is also the last of Ruth Prawer Jhabvala's novels to deal primarily with Indian characters. Her next three novels, *A Backward Place, A New Dominion,* and *Heat and Dust*, take up the interest in

Westerners in India, already introduced in *Esmond in India*. *Get Ready for Battle* is probably Jhabvala's darkest view of modern India; in the ensuing novels she moves from the portrayal of India in her fiction to the portrayal of the Westerner in India, including an interest in India's effect on the Westerner.

Chapter Four
A Clouded Sky
The Later Indian Novels

In her later novels Ruth Prawer Jhabvala turns away from the themes predominating in her earlier works and instead focuses on Europeans in India. *A Backward Place* (1965), as Agarwal, Gooneratne, and others have noted, marks a significant change in the direction of Jhabvala's writing and paves the way for her deeper, more probing studies of India's effects on European characters in *A New Dominion* (1972) and *Heat and Dust* (1975). In 1970 Jhabvala wrote, "I must admit that I am no longer interested in India. What I am interested in now is myself in India" ("Myself in India," 9). These words emphasize the new direction Jhabvala's writing takes in later novels.

For the first time in her fiction Jhabvala also begins to show an interest in the India of the British raj. Clarissa in *A Backward Place* comes from a family that had "had connections with India for ages and ages,"[1] though Clarissa herself is quick to insist that it is not her India. Similarly, in *A New Dominion* Raymond has a family history bound up with India, and the presence of Miss Charlotte also focuses the reader's attention on the past, on Britain's historical relationship with India. In *Heat and Dust* Jhabvala sets half her book—Olivia's story—in the past of the British raj. Similar connections appear in the stories too. When Daphne decides to follow her guru to India, her mother brings "forward several aged relatives who had served in India as administrators during the Raj"[2] to give her advice on clothing, diseases, and so on.

Ten years before the publication of *A Backward Place*, Viddi in *The Nature of Passion* had used that same adjective to describe his country: "'There is very little fashionable life in Delhi,' said Viddi. 'Unfortunately we live in a backward country'" (*NOP*, 140). These sentiments are shared by at least one of the major protagonists of Jhabvala's sixth novel—Etta. *A Backward Place* is concerned with European love and hatred of India. The three major characters, Clarissa, Judy, and Etta, in some respects represent each of the stages (enthusiasm, lack of enthusiasm, hatred) Jhabvala suggests all Europeans living in India go through, but more particularly these three characters can be seen in relation to a remark of Clarissa's early in the novel: "One either merges with Hindu civilization or is drowned by it!" (*BP*, 20).[3] Etta is quick to insist that she is "most definitely definitely one of the drowned ones" (*BP*, 21), and the fact that she (like Esmond) hates Indian food confirms this idea. I would suggest that Clarissa too, despite her enthusiasm, is in this category, while Judy quite unconsciously has merged with Hindu society. Judy is successful where Etta and Clarissa fail because she is denationalized. Judy, Etta, and Clarissa all find themselves living outside their cultural contexts as Europeans in India, but only Judy can merge with— surrender to—her adopted country because only she is willing to shake off the cultural trappings she brought with her and accept those of a new nation.

Jhabvala continues to use contrast as a key element of her writing, and the structure of a novel like *To Whom She Will,* which alternates between scenes within Amrita's family circle and scenes portraying Hari's family, is seen again in this novel as the focus continually shifts from Etta to Judy to Clarissa. The initial description of Judy's home, for example, follows immediately after a description of Etta's home.

Judy's typically Indian home, which recalls Hari's house in *To Whom She Will,* stands in marked contrast to Etta's European-style flat, which is as carefully decorated as Esmond's and frequently after visiting Etta Judy tries to do something to improve her own spartan sitting room. She invariably loses interest, however, and does in fact find her home quite comfortable—more comfortable than the house she had in London. Judy feels secure as well as comfortable in her Indian home, unlike either Etta or Clarissa, who both feel lonely and vulnerable in their own abodes. Judy's feelings of comfort and security are ones shared by Hari Sahni, and eventually by Prem and Indu in *The Householder,* but never by Esmond, who, like Etta and Clarissa (though the latter would vehemently deny it), resists India. Judy's acceptance of her adopted home reflects her acceptance of India and an Indian way of life, while Etta's reference to Judy's attempting "to be an Indian wife in an Indian slum" (*BP*, 27) clearly shows Etta's attitude toward that country and at the same time affirms the reader's view of Judy's attitude. Judy quite correctly points out that "It's not a slum" (*BP*, 27) but indeed a respectable middle-class area. In accepting her home as such, she has adopted Indian values, whereas Etta, firmly holding on to her European values, sees it unfavorably—she "hadn't liked the smell, the noise, the rooms, the children, Bhuaji, and had not hesitated to make this very clear" (*BP*, 27). Clarissa, on the other hand, shows her usual enthusiasm for all things Indian when she visits Judy's home: "'I like it,' she declared. 'It's got character. I do think character in a place is so much more important than anything else, don't you? Now take a place like Etta's—that's got no character at all. No character, no atmosphere'" (*BP,* 129).

Nonetheless, Clarissa's attitude toward the bathroom shows just how deep her enthusiasm really is. Any thoughts she might have had about moving in with Judy are soon dispelled by a brief look at the "rather primitive sort of bathroom" (*BP,* 129). Despite her professed enthusiasm for the simple things in life, Clarissa prefers the elegant surroundings of Mrs. Kaul's well-appointed, Western-style bathroom. As Etta points out, "She likes her comforts, does our Clarissa" (*BP,* 28), and when the time does come for Clarissa to move, she shifts into Etta's comfortable flat.

Judy's acceptance of India is again illustrated by the fact that she wears a sari and ties her hair in a bun, in the fashion of Indian women, and that she arouses no interest in the local bazaars, where she has been fully accepted over the years. The wearing of Indian clothes, particularly a sari, is a sign in Jhabvala's fiction of a character merging with India, a sign that recurs in *A New Dominion, Heat and Dust,* and a number of her short stories. Etta and Clarissa cut entirely different figures, as their dress and the shopping expeditions they undertake show. Etta always dresses immaculately in what she believes to be the latest European styles, shopping only in the smartest shops, and even then keeping herself very aloof. Clarissa, in "her usual Rajasthani peasant skirt" (*BP,* 17)—an enthusiastic but unconvincing attempt to adopt Indian dress—attracts even more attention than Etta. Indeed, when she meets Mrs. Hochstadt in the bazaar, it is not Mrs. Hochstadt, dressed like a typical memsahib, who arouses interest but the bohemian Clarissa, who despite her years in India still fails to understand the first thing about shopping in the bazaars. And while Clarissa professes to love India and everything Indian, her angry, violent reaction to the small boys who pester her suggests the contrary. Plainly, Clarissa will be no more able to merge with Indian civilization than her friend Etta will be.

Judy is the only European character in Jhabvala's novels who speaks fluent Hindustani (Professor Hoch and Esmond may think they do, but neither is easily understood by Indians when attempting to speak that language); this attribute further suggests Judy's sense of belonging in India. Neither Etta nor Clarissa is able to speak an Indian language, and neither appears to have made any attempt to learn one, even though in

Etta's case she has been married to three Indians. It is ironic that Etta
should ask Judy why she stays on in India. Judy has reason to remain; her
family is Indian and she is happy there. Etta has neither family nor
happiness to keep her in India, but she is also painfully aware that she has
nothing awaiting her anywhere else either. The question she asks Judy is
perhaps self-reflexive, and there are other times too when Etta's criti-
cisms of Judy are really self-criticisms.

The sky is a recurrent image, not only in this book but in all Jhabvala's
fiction, even her first novel, *To Whom She Will*. But in *A Backward Place*
it takes on greater significance and will in *Heat and Dust* become a
controlling metaphor. With the growing incidence of European characters in her novels, however, the sky, which is used to reflect the love or
hatred of India felt by the various European characters, becomes an
increasingly negative image.

Jhabvala herself shows two very different responses to the sky in
"Myself in India." In her first response she writes, "India swallows me up
and now it seems to me that I am no longer in my room but in the
white-hot city streets under a white-hot sky" ("Myself in India," 14).
Here the sky is a negative image, "white-hot" and unfriendly. This is the
sky of the third stage of the cycle she describes in that essay. Her second
response is quite different: "And over all this there is a sky of enormous
proportions—so much larger than the earth on which you live, and often
so incredibly beautiful, an unflawed unearthly blue by day, all shining
with stars at night, that it is difficult to believe that something grand and
wonderful beyond the bounds of human comprehension does not ema-
nate from there" ("Myself in India," 15–16). This is the sky of the first
stage of Jhabvala's cycle, clearly reflecting love for India and the ability to
merge. The negative response to the sky is found when the heat from the
sky is felt. The positive view comes from the sight of the sky.

While Jhabvala herself may experience different responses to the sky,
Etta's, Clarissa's, and Judy's responses are consistent throughout *A
Backward Place* and clearly illustrate their feelings for India. Etta's strong
reaction to the sky ultimately portrays her hatred of India. Early in the
novel we are shown the view from Etta's terrace: "Most prominent of all
was the sky, which covered and dwarfed everything, was electric blue and
had black kites wheeling slowly round and round against it" (*BP*, 6).
Usually when Jhabvala's characters see the sky it is as a positive image.
Here, because Judy is the observer, we would expect this to be the case,
and indeed there is the possibility of beauty in this description, but
because the view is from Etta's balcony and because of Etta's presence, the

beauty is compromised by the black kites. The threat the sky offers in this description is reinforced when Etta asks Judy, rhetorically, "Don't you know that the Indian sun has been put specially into the sky to ruin our complexions?" (*BP,* 7). Similarly, at the end of the novel as Etta lies in bed recovering from her attempted suicide and enjoying the attentions of her new admirer, Mr. Jumperwala, she complains to Clarissa that "Through a chink she could see a bit of too blue sky and the black wings of some birds of prey flashing against it" (*BP,* 186). The blue sky might well have been beautiful, but the ominous black wings dominate Etta's view of it, and she can relax only when the curtains have been firmly closed, throwing her room once more into a dimness that excludes India. She is attempting to shut out not only the heat but also the dust: outside her flat "lay the dusty landscape, the hot sun, the vultures, the hovels and shacks and the people in rags that lived there till some dirty disease carried them off" (*BP,* 171). That the dust of the landscape and the heat of the sun are oppressive is stressed here by the mention of vultures and hovels that contrast with the chic interior of Etta's flat. In all three of the quotations just cited birds of prey dominate the sky, and this to Etta is always threatening. She never sees the beauty of the sky; it is the sun's heat and the dust of the landscape that make an impression on her. Here the third stage of the cycle is confirmed not only by heat of the sun, as it was in "Myself in India," but also by the dust of the landscape, which, of course, looks ahead to the title of Jhabvala's eighth novel, *Heat and Dust.*

Clarissa's idealized picture of India, her superficial enthusiasm for that country, is seen in her romantic view of the sky: "Let's go out—fresh air, the sky, the moon, the stars, romance!" (*BP,* 38) she implores Etta and Guppy. Unlike Etta, Clarissa wants to see the beauty of the sky and actively looks for it, but what she sees suggests that India is not what she imagines it is, and that, despite her enthusiasm, it is the wrong place for her: "It was not as nice on the terrace as Clarissa had expected. It was quite dark by now, and there was no moon, and no stars either" (*BP,* 38–39). Again, when she moved into Etta's flat, Clarissa looked at her belongings piled up on the balcony, "and then looked up at the sky and hoped it wouldn't rain" (*BP,* 185). For Clarissa the sky is either indifferent or mildly threatening—the second stage of the cycle.

Judy's reaction to the sky, however, is quite different. To her it is friendly, a source of comfort, thus reflecting her love for her adopted country. Indeed, it is frequently seen as an image of her happiness: "looking up at the sky which was full of moon and thickly sprinkled with stars, she was filled with a sense of trust and happiness that was far beyond any particular cause she could have named" (*BP,* 64). In marked contrast to Clarissa's empty sky, the sky Judy sees is filled with the moon and stars her friend had searched for. When Judy is torn between her desire to stay in Delhi, secure in the family home, and Bal's wish to go to Bombay, she turns to her English past for comfort. But to cling to England would be to drown in India, and Judy realizes this as she gazes at the sky:

yet always, above everything, the sky was large and beautiful, and one had only to look up and it was peaceful. She looked up now and found the sky, in its first dawn of night, a smooth soft surface of pale silver. The old trees were black silhouettes and you could see each leaf quite still and very delicate against the silver.

She couldn't ever remember having looked up at the sky in England. She must have done, but she couldn't remember. There had been nothing memorable: nothing had spoken. So one locked oneself up at home, all warm and cosy, and looked at the television and grew lonelier and lonelier till it was unbearable and then one found a hook in the lavatory. Judy could not imagine ever being that lonely here. In the end, there was always the sky. (*BP,* 179)

This passage is central to an understanding of Judy; at this point she realizes England is no longer her real home and makes her unconscious decision to surrender finally and completely to India, expressed outwardly in her decision to go to Bombay. Judy's memory of the English sky is consistent with Jhabvala's portrayal of England, even from her first novel, *To Whom She Will.* In that novel Krishna Sen Gupta reflects on the time he spent in England and "remembered England now only as a brown place, where one could not sit under the stars" (*TWSW,* 225). The home in Delhi to which Judy had clung "seemed a trivial cause to tie one down in a world which was so wide, encompassed by a sky out of which perhaps someone spoke" (*BP,* 179). This view of the sky, symbolizing her love for India, shows the first stage of the cycle, and because Judy responds to the sky in this way she escapes the heat and dust that plague Etta's India.

Thus their impressions of and responses to the sky show the differing feelings of love and hatred that each of the three main characters has for India.

Similar feelings of love and hatred are evident to varying degrees in other characters in the novel too. On an exchange visit from England the Hochstadts (who share much in common with earlier experts on Indian culture, Professor Hoch in *To Whom She Will* and Esmond of *Esmond in India*) find everything about India charming, but their apparent love is superficial and exists only because they are secure in the knowledge that they will be returning to their cozy flat in St. John's Wood at the end of their two years, a fact setting them apart from the other European characters, Etta, Clarissa, and Judy. There is a great deal of irony in the closing words of the book, which relate to the Hochstadts' experience of India: "But what a store-house of memories they would be taking with them! How greatly they felt themselves enriched by their contact with this fabled land!" (*BP*, 189). In truth they have had very little contact with India; they have lived in India but always apart from it, mixing only with the likes of Mrs. Kaul and Etta. Mrs. Hochstadt's attitude to the beggars of India sums up the Hochstadts' attitude to India as a whole: "She and Franz had discussed the problem of beggars too, and had come to the conclusion that it was no use giving any of them anything. If one wished to be charitable, there were certain charitable organizations to whom one could send a cheque at Christmas or Diwali or some such time of national rejoicing" (*BP*, 73–74). Like the bulk of Europeans, mostly Britons, who spent their time in India during the days of the British raj, the Hochstadts are interested only in what they can take from India and beneath the masks of enthusiasm they constantly wear, have no genuine desire to give anything in return. Were they to remain in India, they would undoubtedly be drowned by that country, and their superficial love would inevitably sour.

Through the Hochstadts Jhabvala exposes her continuing interest in Forster's *A Passage to India*. A fleeting reference had already been made to Forster's novel in *Esmond in India*, and in *A Backward Place* it is taken up once more. Early in the novel Jhabvala describes the view from Etta's balcony in a tone distinctly reminiscent of Forster:

And it was only when one stepped out of the living-room of this top-floor flat on to the terrace (as Judy now did, for Etta was being a long time in her bath) and looked over the parapet, that it became very clear that this was not Europe. The houses, true enough, were built from jazzy pictures in European or American magazines, but the surrounding landscape was not really consonant with anything those magazines might know of. Vast barren spaces, full of dust and bits of litter, flowed around and between the smart new houses; there was not a tree in sight, and the only growth to spring spontaneously out of this soil was, here and there, little huts patched together out of mud and old boards and pieces of sacking. The whole area was intersected by a railway line for goods trains, and there were two prominent landmarks: an old mausoleum of blackened stone and no architectural value (but with a curious air of permanence about it: one felt that when all the pretty houses and all the makeshift huts had gone, this at any rate would still be here), and an enormous brightly coloured advertisement hoarding for rubber tyres. Most prominent of all was the sky, which covered and dwarfed everything, was electric blue and had black kites wheeling slowly round and round against it. (*BP,* 6)

This passage displays the irony that runs through Jhabvala's fiction and is so much a part of Forster's style too. It recalls the opening paragraphs of *A Passage to India* and suggests the strong influence that novel was beginning to have on Jhabvala's writing. Both this passage and the opening paragraphs of Forster's novel mention ancient landmarks that have no architectural value (very recurrent in all Forster's novels and increasingly recurrent in Jhabvala's later ones) and modern edifices that are incongruous with the landscape, which in both passages is cut in two by a railway line. Both descriptions point to the fluid permanency of the mud huts, which disappear and reappear with the changing of the seasons. But perhaps most significantly, the references to the sky in the opening paragraphs of Forster's novel, and which continue throughout *A Passage to India,* are echoed in this excerpt from *A Backward Place.* Moreover, in *A Backward Place* Dr. Hochstadt is able to summon the ghost of *A Passage to India* when he explains to Etta that "Life plays itself out to a different rhythm here" (*BP,* 26), a comment that opens the way for Mrs. Hochstadt's direct reference to Forster's Indian novel and makes it apparent that by the mid-1960s the India of *A Passage to India* had become far more than "another literary landscape" to Jhabvala:[4] "'The echo of the Marabar caves,' said Mrs. Hochstadt. They were cultured people and had of course prepared themselves thoroughly before coming out to India. 'How does it go—boum, boum'" (*BP,* 27). The irony here is double-edged: while *A Passage to India* will prepare no one thoroughly for that country, Jhabvala also concedes that no Western writer is fully prepared for writing about India without having read Forster's novel, and perhaps responding to it—as such writers as J. G. Farrell (in *The Siege of Krishnapur*) and Paul Scott (in the *Raj Quartet* and elsewhere) have also recognized. *A Passage to India* is a prime text in the Anglo-Indian canon, and all writers, European and Indian, who write about British India do so in the shadow of Forster. His novel has had so strong an influence on the way readers—particularly Western readers but Indian readers too—see India that it cannot be ignored. Jhabvala shows she is aware of this point when she confronts *A Passage to India* head-on in *A New Dominion* and *Heat and Dust.*

While in *A Backward Place* Jhabvala is concerned primarily with Europeans in India, there are still a number of important Indian characters, including Sudhir, Bhuaji, Mrs. Kaul, and Bal.

Sudhir, like Krishna Sen Gupta in *To Whom She Will,* is thoroughly dissatisfied with aspects of his mother country as a result of his education. Despite his success at college, Sudhir had spent two years looking for a job because his family lacked the right sort of connections. He was forced to adopt the Indian method of finding work, constantly waiting outside the offices of so-called great men in the hope of finding preferment. (Judy too had been forced to adopt such methods in her search for employment, methods that were described from the other side in *The Nature of Passion,* wherein various supplicants dance attention on Lalaji.) Sudhir's dissatisfaction stems from his modern, emancipated thinking, which is inevitably at odds with the tradition-bound society in which he has to live, and from his genuine concern for the backwardness of his country, a concern he shares with Narayan of *Esmond in India* (in whose footsteps he follows when he too moves to the wilds of Madhya Pradesh) and Guatam of *Get Ready for Battle.* His friend Jaykar, the old revolutionary freedom fighter, is right when he insists that the Cultural Dias is the wrong place for Sudhir to spend his days. But Sudhir has not only strong ideals but a practical side that earlier idealists like Ram Nath have lacked. He knows he must sacrifice his ideals in order to fulfill his responsibilities toward his mother and his unmarried sisters. Only after the death of his mother and the marriages of his sisters is he free to risk his security, follow the directions of his ideals, and go to teach in Madhya Pradesh as Jaykar urges. As a pessimist and a cynic, Sudhir is also used by Jhabvala to provide a contrast to the ever-optimistic and -enthusiastic Bal, Judy's husband.

Bhuaji, the most traditional figure in the novel, is another contrast with Sudhir. Because she is so thoroughly a part of Hindu civilization, she faces none of the problems or frustrations with which Sudhir must contend and is in many ways the most self-contained and the happiest figure in the book. Bhuaji's willingness to go to Bombay with Judy and Bal is an important factor in Judy's decision to agree to leave Delhi. Bhuaji is a positive figure whose nature is valued by Judy. In this she is rather different from earlier widowed relations in Jhabvala's joint-family households, such as Phuphiji in *The Nature of Passion,* whose role is basically negative. Whereas Phuphiji is frequently critical of the younger members of Lalaji's household, Bhuaji is always prepared to see the good in people.

Mrs. Kaul, the latest in Jhabvala's long line of committee women, bears considerable resemblance to her immediate predecessor, Mrs. Bhatnagar of *Get Ready for Battle,* but is a more complex figure. While both women are sharply satirized, Mrs. Kaul is also occasionally seen in a sympathetic light. Her role at the Cultural Dias obviously attracts Jhabvala's satiric pen, as does her condescending attitude toward Sudhir's Bengali friends and Jaykar; she welcomes only "important" visitors to the Cultural Dias. Similarly, her treatment of the girl who has been dismissed from her job as secretary to the Social Development Board reminds both Sudhir and Judy of their own tenuous positions and how they too could be, and in Judy's case have been, dismissed to make way for somebody's son or niece. Yet Mrs. Kaul is basically an unhappy person, using the Cultural Dias as an attempt to fill a gap in her own life, as Tarla Mathur does with the various committees she sits on in *To Whom She Will.* (On one of Mrs. Kaul's committees there is a Mrs. Mathur who could be Tarla—an instance of intertextuality within Jhabvala's own work.) Mrs. Kaul thus attracts our sympathy, as she attracts Sudhir's when he informs her that he will be leaving the Cultural Dias.

Bal, Judy's rather vain husband, is a would-be actor whose talent is unlikely to enable him to fulfill his dream of becoming a successful actor in the mold of his hero and supposed friend Kishan Kumar. Although Bal (like his friends) aspires to emulate Kishan Kumar, we know and Judy knows that he is unlikely to succeed and that his move to Bombay will not bring him the fame and fortune he craves. Indeed, Judy is frightened by Bal's determination to leave the comfort and security of the family home in Delhi and the relative financial security of Judy's job at the Cultural Dias (and the savings she hoards) in order to risk all in the turbulent film world of Bombay. Surprisingly perhaps, Judy's fears are not shared by Sudhir, Jaykar, or Bhuaji, because they have all surrendered to India in a way that, until she agrees to go to Bombay with Bal, Judy has not done.

Love and hatred of India are reflected in the various characters' happiness or unhappiness and in their willingness or unwillingness to merge with Hindu society. Of the three major European characters, Judy alone accepts her adopted country and appears contented; her relationship is finally one of love for India, shown all along by her love and acceptance of Bal. Etta's hatred, in contrast, is shown by her three failed marriages and through her deliberate attempts to separate herself as far as possible from the society in which she is forced to live. Between these two poles is Clarissa, who, though she shows an enthusiasm that Judy never expresses, loves India only superficially. While Clarissa's love of the country as an ideal may continue in its own limited way for some time, she will never accept India in the way Judy has, and, as the signs suggest—her condescending attitude toward Indians that surfaces from time to time—she will in the end find her enthusiasm for India turning sour.

Six years later Jhabvala in "Myself in India" wrote that "To live in India and be at peace one must to a very considerable extent become Indian and adopt Indian attitudes, habits, beliefs, assume if possible an Indian personality. But how is this possible? And even if it were possible—without cheating oneself—would it be desirable?" ("Myself in India," 16). Clarissa's attempts suggest that it isn't possible, and Etta believes that it is most definitely not desirable. But Judy shows, on the contrary, that it may be possible and perhaps also that it can be desirable, though admittedly she has to make considerable sacrifices—sacrifices that neither Clarissa nor Etta is prepared or desires to make. Jhabvala revels in ambiguities that are presented and then left for the reader to accommodate. She does not oversimplify or too neatly tie up her endings, particularly in later novels, and thus avoids final judgments.

A New Dominion and *Heat and Dust* are more complex than any of Ruth Prawer Jhabvala's earlier novels. The symbol of food, discussed in relation to *To Whom She Will,* is important once more in *A New Dominion* as an indication of the way characters are judged (Lee, for example, relishes Indian food and eats even the hottest chilies, which suggests her willingness to adopt Indian values), and the symbols of the sky and clothing are used again in both novels to suggest the natures of various characters. But more important, both novels are concerned with those whom the author describes in one of her collections of stories, *A Stronger Climate,* as "seekers." A major theme is the traditional quest: Lee, Margaret, and Evie in *A New Dominion* are described in the list of characters as "girls on a spiritual quest." The narrator of *Heat and Dust* is a similar figure whom Yasmine Gooneratne refers to an "an archetypal quest-figure."[5]

In *A Backward Place* Jhabvala suggests, through Judy, that it is possible for some Europeans to merge with India and to survive. Again in these two later novels she portrays Westerners who remain in India and survive, as Miss Charlotte does and as both Olivia and the narrator in

Heat and Dust appear to do, though the question of whether this outcome is desirable remains typically unanswered.

These final two Indian novels also differ from Jhabvala's earlier work in that (a) for the first time (except for Esmond's brief excursion to Agra) they move out of Delhi and (b) they employ wholly different narrative techniques—both of which differences Jhabvala attributes to the influence of her film work.[6] Of particular interest here is the multiple narration, skillfully used by the author to provide more than one perspective. Much of *A New Dominion* is narrated in the third person, but in many of the sections given over to Lee and Raymond the intimate first person is adopted. On the first occasion this occurs the third-person narrator intrudes and for the first time in Jhabvala's fiction addresses the reader directly: "Raymond had come for different reasons. Here he is writing to his mother; he writes to her about three or four times a week. They have always shared everything."[7] Also for the first time Jhabvala moves away from middle-class Indians in Delhi and writes about Indians of noble birth in a variety of settings, perhaps due to the influence of James Ivory, who had made princely India the subject of a number of his early films. Rao Sahib and Asha in *A New Dominion* are both of royal blood, as is the Nawab in *Heat and Dust.*

A New Dominion opens with a description of the landscape, which again recalls the opening paragraphs of *A Passage to India* and immediately marks Jhabvala's departure from the essentially home-centered novels she had written to this point; all her previous novels open with domestic scenes.

Despite the fact that all the major characters in *A New Dominion* are on a quest of some sort, none of them are sure what they are looking for; in this respect they are lost souls even before the novel begins. The principal character of the story is Lee, the young woman who had come to India "to lose herself in order—as she liked to put it—to find herself" (*ND,* 10). Raymond too is a seeker, but his is a visit "for different reasons" (*ND,* 10), which are never clearly defined; the reader knows he is on leave from his uncle's publishing business, but what he is really looking for, though it is only hinted at, is a comfortable homosexual relationship, something he refuses to admit even to himself. Like Lee, he makes some attempt to immerse himself in India but does so as a tourist and a seeker of culture (much like the Hochstadts). He brings no furniture with him (like the narrator of *Heat and Dust*), much to the disappointment of his servant, and furnishes his flat with Indian handicrafts—unlike Esmond or Etta, who attempt to furnish their flats in a European style. But despite the

Indian trappings, there remained in Raymond's flat "a foreign atmosphere which simultaneously thrilled and intimidated Gopi" (*ND*, 14). The meeting of East and West here is superficial, and Raymond, as the description of his flat suggests, will never penetrate or discover the "real" India. Similarly, Asha, the Indian princess, is always searching (but never satisfied) as she moves from lover to guru and back again. Her quest, accompanied by the ridiculous scenes she creates, is as pathetic and doomed as Raymond's, and in effect they are both seeking the same thing. Gopi, the young Indian in search of little more than his own pleasure, is not developed as a questing figure; rather, he becomes the object of both Raymond's and Asha's quests.

The differing narrative voices serve to emphasize the distinctions between the characters. The parts of Lee's story told in the first person, which are open and honest, reveal a great deal about her. Raymond also uses the first person in his letters home to his mother, but his is a limited viewpoint, as there are certain things he cannot explain or admit to in these letters, including his real reason for being in India. Asha's story is told in the third person, with very little sympathy, while Gopi's is left to be gathered from his appearance in the narratives of others.

Because of Lee's first-person narrative, the reader learns much about her feelings and thoughts: "Margaret hates modern materialism. Of course so do I; that's why we're both here. But I know that Margaret is more serious than I am in her search. Sometimes I don't know that I *am* searching for anything—sometimes I think maybe I'm just floating around, just not doing anything, just running away from things" (*ND*, 37). Lee does, however, later make a conscious decision to surrender to India, and she sees allowing Gopi to make love to her as part of that surrender: "She suffered rather than enjoyed while he lay on top of her. But she was glad to be doing this for him and, at the final moment, thought to herself that perhaps this was part of the merging she had so ardently desired while looking out of the window" (*ND*, 55).

Lee, unlike Raymond, seems to believe that she can only really know India by experiencing it physically, sexually, rather than by understanding it intellectually. Nevertheless, it is being raped by Swamiji that causes Lee to leave the ashram. Swamiji had rationalized his crime in advance: " 'She must be mine completely in heart and soul and—yes, Raymond,' he said, easily able to read his companion's thoughts, 'in body also, if I think it necessary' " (*ND*, 146). But Lee does not accept this view and thus does not surrender completely in the way that Margaret and Evie have done. Indeed, this resistance is shown in her refusal to wear a sari like the other disciples; instead, like Clarissa, she wears a peasant skirt, suggesting she is only willing to go partway toward merging with India.

Each of the three parts of the novel deals with a particular stage of Lee's quest. The Delhi period relates to her uncertain quest for direction, which is influenced partly by her friend Margaret and partly by her conscious decision not to become like Raymond, who is suffering because he will not admit what he is searching for. The time Lee spends in Benaras is concerned with her attempt to become one with India (her spiritual quest) and, more particularly, with the ashram—a period that is initially beautiful but ends in disillusion. The third stage of the book is concerned with Lee's disillusion and her attempt to resist India. But she is not happy in Maupur: "How wrong, how bad this place is for me! To think that I've travelled and travelled and come all this way and now I've ended up here" (*ND,* 215). Yet in the end Lee cannot turn her back on her quest: she realizes that she can no longer wander vaguely around India; nor can she feel a part of the Western world she sees epitomized in Raymond. For Lee all roads lead back to the ashram. She is already changed by her experience of Swamiji, and at the close of the book the reader realizes that by going back to the ashram Lee risks becoming like Evie or Margaret and ultimately destroying herself.

Whereas in *A Backward Place* Jhabvala uses the sky to illustrate her characters' love and hatred of India, in *A New Dominion* she uses it primarily to show whether her characters are suited to India and, in harness with the sky, increasingly introduces the oppressive images of heat and dust. Such depictions may be the result of Jhabvala writing from an increasingly European perspective and a measure of the growing importance of European characters in her fiction. All the significant references to the sky appear in the sections that concern Lee, whose quest is central to the novel.

Jhabvala's first description of the ashram presents a typically negative picture: "The surrounding landscape was flat, bleak, and dusty. The hutments were strictly utilitarian with tin roofs stuck on brick walls that heated up like ovens in the sun" (*ND,* 81). The dust is all the more oppressive because the flat landscape offers no escape, and the heat beating down from the sky completes the picture of a place consumed by heat and dust.

But the ashram can also be viewed positively, and this possibility is clearly shown when Lee looks up at the evening sky: "Over the hutments, over the snake holes, over the flat barren landscape stretched the evening sky—an opalescent texture tinted in the most delicate and unexpected shades of pink, orange, even pale green" (*ND*, 100). Here instead of looking down and seeing the dust and feeling the heat, oppressive and enveloping, Lee looks up and sees the sky, beautiful in comparison to the landscape, offering in that fleeting moment a feeling of release and the possibility of happiness there.

That Lee is unsuited to life in the ashram is more clearly emphasized the longer she remains there. In later descriptions even the sky changes: "All around there is nothing but miles and miles of flat land and flat sky the same colour as the land" (*ND*, 194–95). Because the sky has now lost its texture and color and is only flat and dust-colored, it becomes an extension of the land. Jhabvala is using the negative images of heat and dust to show how the oppression is closing in on Lee. The longer she stays at the ashram, so the chances of her remaining unharmed by her experiences there will diminish.

As Lee walks over to Swamiji's hut before the terrible rape scene, Jhabvala uses the sky, the heat, and the dust to act as a warning both to Lee and to the reader: "The sky was all torn up by these clouds shifting and sailing rather fast as if they were being driven and making everything up there look very disturbed; and on the earth it was disturbed too with little hot winds blowing through the air and blowing up puffs of dust that skimmed the ground and rose and whirled around in spirals and then sank back again" (*ND*, 196). The violence of the sky, which so far has been unusual in Jhabvala's novels, prepares the reader for Swamiji's ensuing violence; there is no escape for Lee, either from the heat and dust as she crosses the ashram or from the rape that is to come. At this point, when Lee has ignored the many chances of escape offered to her, the heat and dust consume her metaphorically. She came to be changed, and by remaining in the ashram she has made that inevitable. The negative picture of India presented through Lee's experience in the ashram is aimed not at India or its culture as a whole but at the holy men (or unholy men) who attempt to take advantage of European spiritual seekers and at those Western seekers themselves, who persist in their attempts to experience India in a particular way; these false gurus and misguided seekers are a corruption of India's culture rather than an intrinsic part of it. After the assault Lee drags herself back to her hut, "feeling wounded and torn" (*ND*, 199) like the sky she had observed on her first journey across the compound that evening. Yet in a way she has achieved the union with India—albeit primarily sexually rather than spiritually—that she had sought all along.

In Maupur, after her withdrawal from the ashram, Lee feels that The Retreat, where she is staying with her friends Raymond, Asha, and Gopi, is bad for her, though the opposite is suggested by Lee's positive or even friendly view of the sky here—"I see the sky and the stars in it" (ND, 215), which is a far cry from the "flat sky" she looked on in the ashram. When Evie and Margaret appear on the horizon, bringing with them the presence of the ashram, Lee's view of the sky changes once more and the landscape is again dominated by negative images: "They looked like a mirage suddenly appearing on the horizon. The sky, the air, and the earth were all dust-coloured, and those two were the only figures on the landscape" (ND, 223). Just how unsuitable life in the ashram is for these three young women is seen in Margaret's illness, and as she accompanies her friend to the hospital Lee's view of the sky is once more threatening: "It was a horrible journey through miles of sun and dust. Whenever I looked up—which I didn't like to do because of the glare—I saw huge black birds hovering in the sky" (ND, 228). Here the threatening black birds are both a warning to Lee and portents of Margaret's impending death.

When Lee is in the hospital with Margaret and Evie, however, another view of the sky suggests the alternatives still open to her: "The only ventilation in that store-room was from a tiny open grille; someone had hung a piece of sacking in front of it to keep out the heat and glare. When I felt very desperate, I stood on a box and pushed aside that piece of sacking to look out. . . . I liked doing this especially at dusk when the sky went soft as silk and with the strangest lights in it and how beautiful it looked stretched out behind the rugged walls of the fort" (ND, 230). The prison metaphor is obvious—the tiny storeroom resembles a cell; the heat and glare, her oppressive jailers. But the prison she really has to fear is the one governed by Swamiji. Thus the storeroom is also a symbol of the ashram, complete with Margaret and Evie, the oppressive heat and glare replacing the domineering swami. The friendly sky, "soft as silk" and stretching out to the horizon, contrasts sharply with their present conditions and continues to offer the possibility of liberty, the possibility of seeing India as a tourist and returning home still relatively undamaged by her experiences.

But once again Lee ignores this alternative, and the reader knows at the end of the novel that Lee will return to the ashram, a journey of "endless hours of monotonous landscape; heat and dust" (ND, 253). This idea of a journey through heat and dust is negative, and Lee's journey is likely to lead not only back to the ashram but also to a fate similar to

Margaret's. Thus in the closing paragraphs of *A New Dominion* Jhabvala firmly establishes the images of heat and dust that provide the title for her next novel.

Swamiji is a particularly nasty example of a guru, if we accept Lee's account of her rape: "He was terrible, terrifying. He drove right on into me and through me and calling me beastly names, shouting them out loud and at the same time hurting me as much as he could" (*ND*, 198). This horrifying experience causes Lee to fondly remember Gopi making love to her in a Delhi hotel room. Swamiji feels he has the right to claim Lee's body, just as he already has complete control of Evie and Margaret: "His eyes were bright as with fever, he ran a broad, pale tongue swiftly round his lips. 'But I want her [Lee] to become ready for me again. She must come to me as she did at first; with her hands joined, begging for me to take her. And I will take her, and we shall start again from the beginning. But this time we shall go further. I will take her far, very far, right to the end if need be and this time, Raymond, this time there will be no running away'" (*ND*, 209). But it must be considered here whether Swamiji really believes that Lee, Evie, Margaret, and the others have benefited from their experiences with him at the ashram or whether he is being condescending toward them and blatantly cruel. Jhabvala appears to resist making any authorial judgments about Swamiji; rather, she leaves it to the reader to consider this complicated question. To go further than he did last time, Swamiji is presumably prepared to utterly destroy Lee, as he destroyed Margaret, whose death is a direct result of his attitude toward her illness. By the end of the novel, though, as Lee's thoughts begin to draw her back to the ashram and to Swamiji, she realizes that Margaret has been taken "right to the end": "In her present mood, it seemed to her that Margaret was not to be pitied. Margaret had accomplished something, she had gone all the way" (*ND*, 251)—she had accepted Swamiji without holding anything back. Her communication with India, and perhaps the only communication Lee can expect to achieve when she returns to the ashram, is expounded in Swamiji's parable of the dying dog:

A stray dog had been found lying injured near the ashram. It was in a very bad state and cried and cried and touched our hearts to pity. Lee especially was very much affected. She wanted to have it put out of its misery. But Swamiji would not allow it. The dog howled all night. She went again to Swamiji and begged for his permission but again he would not grant it. He said the dog would be dead in the morning. And so it happened. But Swamiji saw that Lee was still very much upset so he explained the whole matter to her. He said "Everything must be experienced to the end. This is true for a dog as for a man as for a bud on a tree. Everything must unfold and ripen. There is sunshine and gentle breezes and there is rain and bitter storms. We must accept and enjoy, or accept and endure, as the case may be. Because we need both enjoyment and endurance, both sun and storm, so that we may ripen into our fullest possibility. Isn't it wonderful that even a dog should be allowed to grow into such ripeness! And if for a dog, then how much more so for a human being!" (*ND*, 158–59)

What Swamiji demands, what he expounds in this disturbing parable, is utter and unquestioning acceptance from his followers.[8] Looked at from a limited, Western viewpoint (that presented by Raymond in the novel), the experiences of Lee and Margaret are wholly negative and Swamiji wholly evil. But in India as elsewhere, there is no simple division between good and evil, as Raymond himself (like Jhabvala) is aware; viewed from Margaret's own perspective, she did find what she was looking for and experienced it to the full, as Lee finally recognizes, even though we as readers do not necessarily allow ourselves to sympathize with her too strongly or to see the sympathetic side of Swamiji too clearly, again like Raymond. For Jhabvala's characters communication on a false level offers nothing the West cannot offer.

Raymond and Asha, though quite unlike Swamiji, are also often harshly presented. Their individual relationships with Gopi show them both to be pathetic people, in search of a happiness they will never find—partly, in Raymond's case, because he will never be honest with himself and admit what he is looking for.

Raymond's quest operates on the level of a subtext to Lee's. His search, which is for homosexual fulfillment, is never completed, but ironically it turns out to be Raymond and not Lee who understands Swamiji and who, albeit on a superficial level, gets along with him. On the other hand, Lee's search, which she sees as a spiritual quest, manifests itself in sexual adventures with both Gopi and Swamiji. And the conclusions to Raymond's and Lee's quests are quite different too. Lee by remaining in India may be fulfilled but will also be changed in time; Raymond, while he may not have found the satisfaction he sought, by returning to England survives relatively unaffected by his experience. Despite his interest in Indian culture, Raymond has kept himself apart from India, as he admits in one of his letters to his mother when he describes his proposed trip around India by air and justifies his mode of transport with these words: "I want to be a tourist—I *am* a tourist—and get quickly from one place

to another without having to take in great draughts of India on the way"
(*ND,* 77). For Raymond his India is epitomized by Gopi: "everything he
loved in Gopi and everything he loved in India. These two were now
inextricable" (*ND,* 47). Thus it is significant that Raymond adopts
Indian clothing only when he is with Gopi and that on other occasions he
stands out in his English clothes—as when his Pembroke College tie is
noticed by the Rao Sahib, and when at the ashram "He was . . . the
only one besides Miss Charlotte who was not wearing Indian clothes"
(*ND,* 179).

Unlike Lee, Raymond heeds warnings against pursuing his quest to its
conclusion. Lee ignores Margaret's death and at the end of the novel
prepares to return to Swamiji and the ashram, and presumably to the
possibility of suffering the same fate as her friend. Raymond, however, as
Yasmine Gooneratne explains, accepts the warnings voiced by Asha, who
tells him about her brother's English tutor's love for a young Indian
clerk. When she later tells him that the tutor, whose feelings were not
reciprocated, had tried to kill himself, Raymond realizes he is in danger
of being overwhelmed by his feelings and hastily makes final arrange-
ments to return to England (Gooneratne, 187–88).

Asha is a remnant of princely India, dissolute and out of place in the
India in which she lives. Like Raymond, she is drawn to Gopi by his looks
and innocence. Her sense of discomfort in modern India is shown by the
way she moves from one house to another, from one city to another, and
from lover to guru and back. Her discomfort is more forcefully illustrated when at the end of the novel she takes to her bed and, like Etta,
closes the curtains in an attempt to shut out India. Her brother, the Rao
Sahib, copes better with the loss of power—an ex-ruler, he now rushes
around the country campaigning for political power to replace the
inherited power of which he has been stripped.

Gopi is another study of a young Indian from a lower-middle-class
Delhi family, in background at least, similar to a number of other such
young men who have appeared in all Jhabvala's novels. Unlike such
characters as Hari Sahni, though, Gopi is taken out of his usual environment, beyond the influence of his family, and is thus able to resist the
marriage his family is arranging for him. The marriage, the reader
surmises, would be far better for him than his rather sordid relationship
with Asha.

Lee, Margaret, and Evie all attempt to merge with India as a necessary
part of their spiritual quests, and all either are or are likely to be changed
if not destroyed by the attempt. Raymond, however, makes no such

attempt to meet India and remains very much a tourist, an observer of Indian culture and history, much like Fielding in *A Passage to India*. These interests separate him from the spiritual seekers, though in the end neither he nor they will fit in in the ways they had hoped. In the context of the quest Raymond's failure to "become Indian" is on one level seen as wrong, but perhaps, after all, Raymond is right, and Westerners should accept their position as tourists in India, as Banubai, the abrasive but genuine Holy Mother suggests: "She talked about foreigners who come to India because they are bored in the West. They pretend to be in search of spiritual values, but because they don't know what true spiritual values are, they fasten themselves on to harmful elements who only help to drive them deeper down into their disturbed egos; and so not only do they themselves suffer bad consequences but also all sorts of poisonous influences are released, polluting the air breathed in by truly spiritual Indians" (*ND*, 203). Indeed, Margaret's reasons for being in India, which Lee explains early in the novel as she analyses her own reasons for being in the country, appear to justify Banubai's words: "She says people just don't come any more to India to do good, those days are over. What they come for now is—well, to do good to themselves, to learn, to *take* from India" (*ND*, 37). This is an important passage. Margaret is deliberately dissassociating herself from the administrators of the British raj. But unintentionally and unobserved by Lee, her words suggest that her reasons for being in India and the reasons of the many seekers like her are entirely selfish, whereas the voice behind the words seems to be suggesting that at least the men and women who came out to serve the raj had notions, though frequently misguided, of serving India. They were prepared to *give*, whereas Margaret and those like her want only to take. This point is emphasized through the character of Miss Charlotte, the elderly missionary who, although she remains as stoically English as Raymond despite her many years in India, is the only Western character who does fit in and the only Western character who is seen to give anything to India. Through her Jhabvala again illustrates that it is at times possible to survive in India. Ironically, Miss Charlotte is the only major nonquesting Westerner in the book and the only figure who knew all along (like Judy) exactly why she was in India.

Miss Charlotte (again like Judy) is clearly a character that the author admires, and it is interesting to note that Miss Charlotte's literary tastes—"her favourite novelists were George Eliot and Thomas Hardy" (*ND*, 21)—correspond to Jhabvala's own as outlined in her Neil Gunn Memorial Lecture, where she states, "The more regional, the more deeply rooted a writer was, the more I loved them: George Eliot, Thomas Hardy, Charles Dickens. Their landscapes, their childhood memories became mine. I adopted them passionately" ("Disinheritance," 7). The underlying message of this shared liking for the novels of Eliot and Hardy may be that both Miss Charlotte and Jhabvala herself prefer a fictionalized, even partly idealized England. Jhabvala is no doubt well aware of this preference for a fictional England and all it implies. Perhaps Jhabvala's decision to move to New York was prompted in part by a feeling (possibly subconscious) that the *real* England, after Jhabvala's 25 years in India, would be disappointing in comparison to the fictional one. Similarly, Miss Charlotte's attitude toward home—which for her can never mean India, regardless of how many years she spends there—also calls to mind the author's attitude toward India as a place that ultimately can never be home: "I have lived in India for most of my adult life. My husband is Indian and so are my children. I am not, and less so every year" ("Myself in India," 9). This last sentence implies that at the beginning Jhabvala felt "almost" Indian. Nationality, then, is perhaps a matter not only of fact but of psychological and physical context. As the years passed it seems that Jhabvala felt increasingly British in India, but very German when she moved to New York.

With the presence of Miss Charlotte, the past takes on greater significance in this novel. She has been in India 30 years—long enough to be in effect a remnant of the British raj. Her visits to dependents of the mission bring the ghost of the past into the present. The role her father played in the relief of Lucknow, for example, is recalled by one elderly woman, while an elderly man Miss Charlotte describes to Raymond in one of her letters "first came to India fifty years ago to be an assistant in Phillips' (a very smart gentleman's outfitter, it closed down in '47)" (*ND*, 169). And Raymond himself, like the narrator of *Heat and Dust*, comes from a family that had ties with India.

Although India has changed considerably—as the title *A New Dominion* implies in one of its deliberately ambiguous meanings—and is no longer the same country that was visited by Adela Quested and Mrs. Moore, Jhabvala's seventh novel shares much with the novel of her illustrious predecessor.

As Ramlal Agarwal and others have noted, a number of Forsterian characters can be found in *A New Dominion*. V. S. Pritchett enunciates this aspect in a review of the novel published in the *New Yorker:* "Forster's and Mrs. Jhabvala's characters are matched. Raymond, the sensitive, spinsterly English aesthete and inquirer, is another Fielding plus unconscious homosexuality; his Indian friend, the ingenuous and ludicrous student Gopi, is in some ways a budding, ill-educated, up-to-date version of Dr. Aziz."[9] And so on. Just as Aziz comes to tea at Government College and Fielding later visits Aziz in his home, so Gopi has tea with Raymond and later Raymond takes tea at Gopi's house. Gopi, like Aziz, feels very much at home when he visits the Englishman, but both Indians are uncomfortable when they are in turn visited by, respectively, Raymond and Fielding. Further, Gopi is the only character in Jhabvala's novels who regularly recites poetry, and he is moved by poetry in the same way as Aziz, who finds solace and spiritual happiness in it. The central questing figure in *A New Dominion,* Lee, must surely be an up-to-date Adela Quested. Her experiences focus the novel, and it is she who, like Adela, wishes to see the real India. Whereas in *A Passage to India* Adela Quested, Mrs. Moore, and Fielding all get involved with Aziz, in *A New Dominion* Lee, Asha, and Raymond all get involved with Gopi. Another chief similarity lies in the characters of Fielding and Raymond. In *A Passage to India* there is that short but significant chapter which brings the "Caves" section to a close, a chapter that describes Fielding's return to England via Italy and compares Fielding's (and Forster's) cultural responses to India and Italy (or East and West). In *A New Dominion* Raymond at one stage wishes to meet his mother in Italy before returning to England; however, the plan is canceled when Raymond finally decides he wishes to return directly home. For Raymond there is no point in stopping in Italy; for him there is no need to compare cultures, as his trip to India was, in the end, only personal, and his lasting memory would be of Gopi, as Forster's would be of H.H. and Syed Ross Masood (the young Indian whom Forster loved and to whom *A Passage to India* is dedicated).

Structure is another area in which similarities exist between the two novels. Both have a tripartite structure—"Mosque," "Caves," and "Temple" in *A Passage to India* and "Delhi," "The Holy City," and "Maupur" in *A New Dominion*—and the corresponding parts of Jhabvala's novel reflect those of Forster's. In "Mosque" and "Delhi" the British are seen on relatively familiar ground, characters are developed, relationships are established, and various meetings occur. Adela's desire to escape the world of Anglo-India is mirrored by Lee's desire to escape the world of modern materialism. In both novels the climax, the so-called assault in the caves and the terrible assault on Lee at the ashram, occurs in the second part. In these sections both Forster's and Jhabvala's characters go in search of their real Indias, to the Marabar Caves and Benaras, respectively, and each finds something very different from what he or she anticipated. Forster's third section sees a shift to the princely state of Mau, while in Jhabvala's final section her characters retreat to Maupur. Surely Maupur, literally the town or city of Mau, is deliberately named—a wry acknowledgment to Forster and the significance of his great novel, and a good example both of the sense of play so integral to postmodern fiction (though *A New Dominion* is not fully a postmodern novel) and of Jhabvala's sense of her connections with Forster (and James too). Jhabvala appears to be deliberately imitating Forster's own witty, self-mocking manner of treating the combined fictional world as inter-referential. A suggestion is made in *A Passage to India* that Mau is the real India,[10] and a similar suggestion is made in *A New Dominion* that Maupur is the real India (*ND, 55*). Further, both Forster and Jhabvala in the final sections of their novels explore the connections between *public* East-West conflicts and *private* East-West conflicts.

The problems of communication, so important to *A Passage to India,* are also dealt with in her own way by Jhabvala, who constantly reminds us that we are culturally influenced. When Lee submits to Gopi, she does so with these thoughts in her mind: "She wished they could be closer together in understanding, that she could explain herself better to him. But perhaps it was not possible by means of words" (*ND, 54–55*). The young questing figures of the 1970s are prepared to go much further in their search for what they see as the real India, and in their search for communication too. When Lee, who (like Harriet in *Three Continents*) is a rather ambiguous figure sexually, gazes out of the window of the hotel room she is in with Gopi, she appears to be at one with the universe:

> Gopi again put his hand where it had been before; again she flicked him off with the same movement as of a practised hand waving away flies. She really didn't notice or care; she was too engrossed in what was outside. Now her eyes had travelled up to the great domes hovering against a sky of a cerulean blue that she had before seen only in paintings depicting the birth or death of Christ. At that moment she had what she thought must be a mystic experience: at any rate, she felt a great desire to merge with everything that was happening out there—to become part of it and cease to be herself. (*ND, 52*)

This spiritual communication, however, lasts only as long as she is free to allow her mind to wander over the rooftops; once her attention is drawn back inside, back to Gopi, that is, the question of communication is returned to a personal level (which is also the level of Banubai's treatment of Gopi and of Swamiji's treatment of each of his followers individually). It is on a sexual rather than spiritual level that Lee encounters India, first through Gopi and later through Swamiji. But like Adela before her, she does not appear to find any answers.

The intimate tone of the first-person narratives in *A New Dominion,* particularly Raymond's letters to his mother but also Lee's story, recalls the letters Forster wrote to his own mother. Indeed, much about Raymond in *A New Dominion*—and Harry in *Heat and Dust* and Cyril Sahib in the film *Autobiography of a Princess* too—recalls Forster. Haydn Williams is right to suggest that "Raymond is a benevolent if somewhat comic version of E. M. Forster," though I find it hard to agree with his suggestion that "Harry may be a malicious caricature of a type of homosexual Englishman in India represented by E. M. Forster and Ackerley of *Hindu Holiday* [sic]."[11] Harry may be a caricature, and perhaps some of Jhabvala's characters are slightly larger than life, but he is not a malicious caricature—we are too aware of his suffering not to sympathize with him. Richard Cronin, who convincingly details the likenesses between Forster and Harry, is also only partly correct when he explains a significant difference between the two: "Harry is utterly without genius. He is a talentless Forster, an Ackerley without wit or social grace, but on that account, Ruth Jhabvala suggests, he is the more trustworthy witness."[12] Jhabvala, it appears, includes the homosexual figures of Raymond and Harry in these two novels partly as a gesture to Forster but also for sound artistic purpose: their homosexuality gives them a kind of objective distance, makes them outside the "normal" perspectives. Jhabvala does not go in for malicious caricatures—she is far too subtle a writer for anything so black-and-white, and in this respect too she is like Forster. As readers we can choose whether or not to identify with Raymond. If we choose to identify with him, a particular reading is formed; if we choose not to, we create a different reading.

Ruth Prawer Jhabvala confronts *A Passage to India* again in her next novel, *Heat and Dust,* which contains two parallel yet distinct stories: the earlier of the two is set in the India of 1923, the India of a still-secure British raj and princely states; the later story, set in the 1970s (1982 in the film), is about a modern, independent India. As the two stories converge and drift apart again, Jhabvala explores the relationships between two Indias separated in time by 50 years, just as she used *A New Dominion* to explore and reflect the concerns of an earlier India, that of Forster's *A Passage to India.*

But Jhabvala does not only compare two Indias in *Heat and Dust;* she again responds to Forster's novel quite deliberately, setting the earlier of her stories in the early 1920s, the period, I believe, that must be accepted as that of Forster's novel (1923, the year in which Olivia's story is set, is the year of Fielding's return to India in part 3 of *A Passage to India*; parts 1 and 2 of Forster's novel take place in 1921). Many critics (including Paul Scott) suggest that Forster's novel is set pre–World War I, but in *A Passage to India* there are many hints suggesting a later setting, such as the reference to the Nawab Bahadur having had a car nine years earlier (Jhabvala's Nawab too drives a car). An even more unmistakable dating occurs when Hamidullah fondly remembers his days in England and taking the young Hugh Bannister to Queen Victoria's funeral (1901), where he held him in his arms above the crowd. He later recalls "How happy he had been there, twenty years ago!" (Forster, 120).

As in *A New Dominion,* a number of Forsterian characters appear in *Heat and Dust.* There are obvious parallels to be drawn between Olivia Rivers and Adela Quested, as well as between Douglas Rivers and Ronny Heaslop, both of whom are magistrates and well regarded by their superiors and the British community in general—as Mr. Turton, the Collector, states, "The long and short of it is, Heaslop's a sahib; he's the type we want, he's one of us" (Forster, 47); Douglas Rivers is held in similar regard by Mr. Crawford. There are also clear parallels between the Nawab and Aziz, particularly in their respective relationships with Olivia and Adela, and between the Turtons and Burtons of Forster's novel and the Callendars and Minnies of Jhabvala's.

Certain events further link the two novels. The Bridge party, held at the club on what was to all intents and purposes British ground, is mirrored in *Heat and Dust* by the Nawab's dinner, held quite emphatically on Indian soil—both social events bring Britons and Indians together, but Jhabvala has subtly shifted the balance of power from one side of the divide to the other. And just as Adela and Mrs. Moore attempt to follow up the Bridge party by visiting the Bhattacharyas in their home (and as Fielding visits Aziz after the tea party at Government College), so the Nawab, after the dinner at Khatm, visits Olivia in her home. But perhaps the most interesting similarity between Jhabvala's novel and Forster's is the way that Olivia's trip to Baba Firdaus's shrine reflects Adela's visit to the Marabar caves. Although Aziz and Adela make only one trip to the caves, that single excursion is effectively divided into two distinct visits to the caves themselves. The initial visit is in the company of Mrs. Moore and sundry attendant followers; the second sees Aziz and Adela resume their sight-seeing alone except for a single guide. Similarly, in *Heat and Dust* Olivia and the Nawab make two visits to the shrine: the first is with a party of followers, including Harry, who fulfills the role occupied by Mrs. Moore during the trip to the Marabar caves. On this occasion the Nawab, like Aziz, has laid out a picnic and arranged for entertainment to keep his English guests amused, and on the second visit the Nawab and Olivia return alone. The significant difference between these excursions and consequently between the stories told by Foster and Jhabvala is that whereas the sexual activity in the caves is only in Adela's mind, Olivia and the Nawab do make love on their second visit to the shrine.

On the surface the structure of *Heat and Dust* appears to have much in common with that of *A Passage to India,* although the dynamics of the two novels are often quite different. Jhabvala is not, after all, simply retelling *A Passage to India.* Jhabvala's story, like Forster's novel, begins on the relatively firm ground of British India (rather than the princely states, though Forster's novel does open with Indian characters, Aziz and his friends, who are discussing the British). Olivia's refusal to accept what for her is the stifling role of an Anglo-Indian memsahib sees her drawn more and more toward Khatm, which for her represents Adela's "real India." The zenith that occurs in the Marabar caves is achieved in Jhabvala's story in the love scene at Baba Firdaus's shrine. In *A Passage to India* the Marabar caves are literally a zenith because Adela and Aziz climb up to them, while metaphorically they are a low point in the novel, the lowest point of disunity and lack of communication, ironically mistaken for sexual conjunction, a high point of unity and communication. Baba Firdaus's shrine is, by contrast, on the plains. It is geographically a low point but metaphorically a high point of unity and communication between Olivia and India before she discovers that she and the Nawab have been misunderstanding each other. There are other structural parallels too. Adela's retraction of her evidence in court and her subsequent flight to Government College are mirrored by Olivia's abortion and her flight to Khatm. Olivia's move up to the town of X, high in the Himalayas, is the equivalent of Adela's return to England. The final section of *A Passage to India,* "Temple," which shifts the action to the princely state of Mau, is not reflected directly in Jhabvala's novel (and it is absent altogether in Santha Rama Rau's dramatized version of *A Passage to India,*)[13] though indirectly it is taken into account in the presence of Khatm.

The question of communication and of the possibility of a meeting of East and West, a meeting of opposites, which is answered negatively by

Forster at the end of *A Passage to India,* is also voiced in *Heat and Dust,* by the naive Olivia: "'Don't look like that, Harry. You're being like everyone else now: making me feel I don't *understand.* That I don't know India. It's true I don't, but what's that got to do with it? People can still be friends, can't they, even if it is in India.' She said all this in a rush; she didn't want to be answered, she was stating her position which she felt to be right."[14]

In many respects Olivia's questioning mirrors Adela's naive questioning early in Forster's novel and also causes the reader to reflect on Aziz's question in the closing paragraphs: "Why can't we be friends now? . . . It's what I want. It's what you want." In that novel the answer is emphatic: "But the horses didn't want it—they swerved apart; the earth didn't want it, sending up rocks through which riders must pass single-file; the temples, the tank, the jail, the palace, the birds, the carrion, the Guest House, that came into view as they issued from the gap and saw Mau beneath: they didn't want it, they said in their hundred voices, 'No, not yet,' and the sky said, 'No, not there'" (Forster, 316). And no one and nothing wanted the relationship between Olivia and the Nawab to continue—neither the British in Satipur nor the Indians in Khatm—but on an individual level and with sacrifices on both sides, Olivia and the Nawab could be, and were, friends, *then* if not *there.*

And there are other passing references too that link Jhabvala's work to Forster's. In *A Passage to India* Ronny comments disparagingly on the presence of a visiting Labour member of Parliament: "It's the educated native's latest dodge. They used to cringe, but the younger generation believe in a show of manly independence. They think it will pay better with the itinerant M.P." (Forster, 54). Jhabvala makes a more specific reference, presumably to that same member of Parliament: "'Culture!' cried Dr. Saunders. 'You've been talking to that bounder Horsham!' Olivia didn't know it but her words had recalled those of an English member of Parliament who had passed through the district the year before and had put everyone's back up" (*HAD,* 58–59).

In *Heat and Dust* Jhabvala also makes what could be a quiet reference to that other seminal British novel of India, Rudyard Kipling's *Kim,* when she refers to an English chaplain who "came from Ambala and held a service in the little church" (*HAD,* 153). In Kipling's novel Umballa (phonetically the names sound alike) is where Kim delivers the message for Mahbub Ali and where he is taken by Mr. Bennett and Father Victor, the two priests, after he has found the Mavericks' camp. In itself this reference is of minor importance, but alongside Jhabvala's interest in *A*

Passage to India it helps establish the earlier of her two stories in the tradition of Anglo-Indian fiction of the period. Indeed, it is surely no coincidence that the names Jhabvala chooses for the major English characters in her 1923 story are Olivia and Douglas. *Olivia in India* by O. Douglas (the pen name used by Anna Buchan, the sister of John Buchan) consists of a series of letters written from India, just as in *Heat and Dust* it is the letters penned by Jhabvala's Olivia that draw the unnamed narrator to India and provide the structure of the earlier story. (Major Minnies's monograph, which the narrator reads, provides a source of internal intertextuality within the novel itself—a source the narrator can refer to in the way Jhabvala draws on earlier texts for her own knowledge of British India in the 1920s.

Jhabvala takes delight in offering to the alert reader a series of literary clues that point to Forster's novel. In both *A New Dominion* and *Heat and Dust* Jhabvala, by responding to *A Passage to India,* deliberately exhibits a postmodernist interest in the effect of text on life, an interest in intertextuality that is further emphasized by the juxtaposition of the two stories in *Heat and Dust.* Within that novel the effect of Olivia's letters on the unnamed narrator of the later story is explored. Jhabvala forces on the reader the recognition that all story is influenced by previous story and provides a richly suggestive echo of the changes and similarities between two different literary periods, as well as between two different times.

Heat and Dust owes much to Forster's *The Hill of Devi,* as Richard Cronin has illustrated in his excellent essay *"The Hill of Devi and Heat and Dust,"* and, I believe, as much again to *A Passage to India.* But while Jhabvala may have turned to E. M. Forster for some of her knowledge of British India, that does not mean she agrees with all Forster's conclusions, and thus in many ways, despite its similarities with Forster's novel, the earlier of the two stories in *Heat and Dust,* Olivia's story, is the story that *A Passage to India* does not tell.

When Jhabvala turns her attention to the past in the earlier of the two stories in *Heat and Dust,* she does so for the first time in her fiction. As the narrator tells the reader at the beginning of the novel, "this is not my story, it is Olivia's as far as I can follow it" (*HAD,* 2). And while this statement should not be taken entirely at face value, it does suggest a deliberate attempt to direct the reader toward Olivia's story and the past. It also suggests that the narrator intends to follow Olivia's story herself. Thus the central action of the later story (unlike that of *A New Dominion*) is clearly defined from the outset. The narrator's quest is to find out about

Olivia's past and to experience as far as possible what Olivia, her grandfather's first wife, experienced 50 years earlier.

From the beginning the unnamed narrator makes a deliberate attempt to merge with India, as the spartan furnishings in her room illustrate: "The only piece of furniture I have so far acquired is a very tiny desk the height of a foot-stool on which I have laid out my papers. . . . It is the sort of desk at which the shopkeepers do their accounts. Inder Lal looks at my bare walls. Probably he was hoping for pictures and photographs— but I feel no need for anything like that when all I have to do is look out of the window at the bazaar below. I certainly wouldn't want to be distracted from that scene. Hence no curtains either" (*HAD*, 6–7). The bare room is a far cry from the carefully decorated, European-style flats Esmond and Etta inhabit, and a far cry too from the ostentatiously Indian flat Raymond lives in. Whereas Etta keeps her curtains firmly closed in an attempt to shut out India, the narrator of *Heat and Dust* chooses to have no curtains and deliberately attempts to become a part of the world Etta excludes.

The narrator's conscious attempt to immerse herself in India is also reflected in the symbols of clothing and the sky. Sleeping in the open courtyard along with the other families who live in the building, the narrator explains, "I no longer change into a nightie but sleep, like an Indian woman, in a sari" (*HAD*, 52). The sari is a frequent symbol in Jhabvala's fiction; the adoption of one suggests that a character has definitely assimilated with India—which is not the case with the baggy trousers and knee-length shirt "such as the Punjabi peasant women wear" (*HAD*, 9) that the narrator earlier chooses to don (or with the Rajasthani peasant skirts worn by Clarissa and Lee). And like Judy in *A Backward Place,* the unnamed narrator reflects on the sky: "Lying like this under the open sky there is a feeling of being immersed in space— though not in empty space, for there are all these people sleeping all around me, the whole town and I am part of it. How different from my often very lonely room in London with only my own walls to look at and my books to read" (*HAD*, 52). Judy also felt she could never be alone in India and remembered the terrible solitude England could inflict.

More frequently in this novel, however, Jhabvala's characters do not look up at the sky; rather, they look down or out at the dust-colored earth, and the sky is felt in the form of the oppressive heat. The narrator, despite her apparent love for India, frequently describes the sky in this way: "If the buses are always the same, so are the landscapes through which they travel. Once a town is left behind, there is nothing till the next one except flat land, broiling sky, distances and dust" (*HAD*, 11). Here on her excursion to Khatm with her landlord, Inder Lal, it is the earth, the "flat land" stretching out ahead of her, that she sees; the sky, described as "broiling," is felt rather than seen. Judy particularly and the narrator earlier had looked at the sky; on this occasion the narrator feels it as does Olivia, the heroine of the 1923 story, most of the time.

Described in this way both sky and earth take on a negative aspect, and Jhabvala's heat and dust must be seen as a negative image. Conversely, the sky remains a positive image when it is seen rather than felt, as is the case when the narrator stops Maji from proceeding with the abortion attempt. As she steps out of Maji's crude hut, "[t]he sky shone in patches of monsoon blue through puffs of cloud" (*HAD*, 165), suggesting that she has taken the right course. And it is the sky Olivia looks to for comfort as she awaits her abortion: "she had a clear view through the window of a patch of sky. She tried to concentrate on that and not on what they were doing to her" (*HAD*, 167).

More than simply a negative image, heat and dust become a metaphor for one India and for the effect that country has on Westerners: the India of the third stage of Jhabvala's cycle, whereas Judy's sky had been the India of the first.

In the earlier story the position of the English in India was obviously very different, and the freedom enjoyed by the narrator of the later story did not exist. Olivia, except in the evenings and on Sundays, "was alone in her big house with all the doors and windows shut to keep out the heat and dust" (*HAD*, 14). In other words, the closed doors exclude India, as Etta's curtains and Jhabvala's blinds do.[15] Again the prison metaphor is apparent. The bungalow becomes for Olivia a prison cell to which she is confined by the heat and dust and, of course, by the customs of British India. An escape from one necessarily means an escape from the other. It is only as she imagines herself in love, first with her visits to Khatm and later with the Nawab himself, that Olivia begins to see beyond the heat and dust that had earlier constituted her view of India, the limited view of the British raj. At the same time, her view of the sky becomes more positive: "Although the way was so hot and dusty, the landscape utterly flat and monotonous, Olivia learned to like these morning drives. Sometimes she glanced out of the window and then she thought well it was not so bad really—she could even see how one could learn to like it (in fact, she *was* learning): the vast distances, the vast sky, the dust and sun and occasional broken fort or mosque or cluster of tombs" (*HAD*, 85). Here Jhabvala initially uses her heat-and-dust metaphor to show that nothing has changed except Olivia's feelings; because the sky is described as "vast" rather than hot or oppressive, it is no longer a negative image, but neither is it a positive one—thus still suggesting that this may not be the best course for Olivia to take.

As her visits to Khatm continue, Olivia does begin to see the sky in a positive way—but always in Khatm; beyond its walls her outlook is still dominated by negative images: "She went to the window. The sun was beating down of course—the gold dome of the Nawab's mosque gave out blinding beams—but the lawns were sparkling green and the fountains, refracting the sun's rays, dazzled with light and water. In the distance, beyond the pearl-grey Palace walls, lay the town in a miserable stretch of broken roofs, and beyond that the barren land: but why look that far?" (*HAD*, 103). For Olivia India and the Nawab become inseparable; for her the sky is a positive image only when he is close or in her thoughts. Heat, then, is also used as a symbol of passion in this novel. Olivia remains in Satipur when the hot weather arrives because she doesn't want to leave Douglas ("We haven't been—together so very long" [*HAD*, 32], she shyly tells Mrs. Crawford) and also because of her growing passion for the Nawab. This is obviously a dangerous passion, and thus her drives to Khatm are through the dust as well as the heat.

It is inaccurate and unfair to say, then, that the heat and dust Jhabvala certainly sees in India have destroyed her ability to see the beauty of that country. Jhabvala's heat and dust may indeed constitute a negative image, but that does not mean she presents India only in a negative light. The sky provides a positive use also, to balance this image, and shows that Jhabvala sees the good as well as the bad side of the country she lived in for 25 years.

Heat and Dust examines a far greater and more varied range of English characters than can be found in any of Jhabvala's earlier novels. In previous novels Jhabvala has looked at the effects of India on seekers like Lee, Clarissa, Etta, or even Esmond, and she has considered the position of characters like Judy and Miss Charlotte in a modern India. But in *Heat and Dust* her range expands; she explores the effects of India on seekers like the young narrator, on the missionary lady the narrator meets in Bombay and the derelicts outside A's Hotel, and on long-term residents in the days of the British raj. It may well be, as Yasmine Gooneratne posits, that "Ruth Jhabvala is externalising and probing through fiction certain aspects, painful, exhilarating, puzzling and comic, of her own experience of India (Gooneratne, 211).

Although they are all questing figures, the difference between the narrator of *Heat and Dust* and the three young women of *A New Dominion* is seen quite clearly when the former meets the three English travelers who were all originally attracted to India for spiritual reasons. Chid in particular is like Lee and her friends. Like them, he adopts Indian clothing, the Hindu religion, and even an Indian name (equivalent to the new name with which an Indian convert is christened on baptism)—though comically he never loses his "flat Midlands accent" (*HAD,* 20). In the end, though, Chid rejects all this and does what Lee finds she cannot do: he goes home, thus showing how difficult it can be to merge with or surrender to India and also—frequently—how undesirable it is to do so.

Chid's resolve to leave India appears to prompt the narrator's resolve to stay, which she knows she must do if she is to fulfill her quest: "More and more I want to find out; but I suppose the only way I can is to do the same she did—that is, stay on" (*HAD,* 160). Her decision to leave Satipur and go up into the mountains symbolically shows this resolve and, of course, parallels Olivia's own move. Unlike Chid, who leaves Satipur because, as Maji puts it, "He had to run away" (*HAD,* 173), the narrator is going farther and probing deeper into India, and her pregnant condition will make it increasingly difficult for her to come down from the mountains, to turn her back on her quest, and perhaps, like Chid, on India.

The narrator, like Judy, appears to merge with India successfully, possibly because she, like Judy and Miss Charlotte, has a purpose for being in India and is prepared to accept India as it is, to surrender herself to India without needing to throw off her own identity. Like her previous avatars and like many of the raj figures of the 1923 story, the narrator learns to swim in the flowing tide of India—unlike Etta or Chid, who drown there. It is possible that, like Major Minnies (who is a comparable character to Dr. Hochstadt, though more sympathetically portrayed), some of those characters who survive in India do so because they learn to love India in a particular way: "Yes, concluded the Major, it is all very well to love and admire India—intellectually, aesthetically, he did not mention sexually but he must have been aware of that factor too—but always with a virile, measured, *European* feeling" (*HAD,* 171).

A skillful interplay of corresponding characters and events exists between the two stories in *Heat and Dust,* which, like *A Passage to India* and *A New Dominion,* are separated by 50 years. Obviously, the unnamed narrator is a modern-day Olivia; Inder Lal, the figure who resembles the Nawab; Chid and his companions, the new Douglas Rivers and the Anglo-Indian community of Satipur; and so on. The events of the two stories progress side by side too, interwoven even more closely by the frequent time shifts Jhabvala employs, a technique she has learned from her writing for the cinema and one she uses with consummate skill here. In particular, Jhabvala has adapted many of the technical devices she used in *Autobiography of a Princess.* In her screenplay for that film two time periods similar to those used in *Heat and Dust* are interwoven. The present is London in the 1970s, where the princess recovers the past through documentary footage of royal India in the 1920s. In *Heat and Dust* Olivia's journals take the place of the documentary film clips.

Unlike Jhabvala's earlier novels, which had a single, identifiable narrative voice, *Heat and Dust,* like *A New Dominion,* has a structure that allows for many viewpoints, and the characters in these latter two novels are seen from different angles by different people. In *Heat and Dust* the narrator's story is told throughout in the first person, thereby bringing readers close to her feelings. Olivia's story, though told in the third person, is taken directly from her journals and letters, which again gives a feeling of intimacy. When, however, Olivia has the abortion that effectively marks her decision to leave Douglas and flee to Khatm and the Nawab, the mode of the narration changes. Her journals cease, and her later letters, we are told, become less vivid and less detailed; consequently, the narrator has to rely on what others tell her about the final stages of Olivia's life. At this juncture the 1923 story becomes part of the narrator's, separated from hers only by the different narrative voices, and this intermingling of the stories suggests the narrator's own blending with Olivia's and the successful fulfillment of the narrator's quest.[16]

The parallel stories do much to create a sense of history in this novel, each story lending a definite sense of time to the other. Much of the contemporary Western, predominantly European interest in India is a legacy of the period of the British raj, as the use of the 1923 story shows. Although *Heat and Dust* could never be described as a historical novel, the 1923 story in particular evinces a strong sense of history. While the year is clearly identified from the opening page of the novel, the zeitgeist of the period is captured in other, more subtle ways. Everything Jhabvala writes about in the 1923 story suggests that period. Olivia's worries about the future a child of theirs might have in India, for instance, and Douglas's confident reply plainly voice some of the concerns of the Anglo-Indian community of that time: "'Supposing things change—I mean, what with Mr. Gandhi and these people'—but she trailed off, seeing Douglas smile behind her in the mirror. *He* had no doubts at all, he said 'They'll need us a while longer,' with easy amused assurance" (*HAD,* 89). The reference to Gandhi, whose role in the freedom movement was very active by this time, combined with the fact that India's independence is still only a possibility to Olivia and hardly even that to Douglas—all add up to suggest the early 1920s.

As far as the English community in Satipur is concerned, Olivia has all the makings of a typical memsahib, as Beth Crawford's words, which Douglas recounts to Olivia, express: "She said she was sure that someone as sensitive and intelligent as you are—you see she does appreciate you, darling—that you would surely be . . . all right here. That you—well, this is what *she* said—that you'd come to feel about India the way we all do" (*HAD*, 26). But Olivia (like Adela Quested) has no desire to become another typical memsahib; to do so, she feels, would separate her from what she imagines is the "real India"—though she never publicly expresses the wish to see the "real India," as Adela naively does in Forster's novel.

Olivia's life in Satipur offers little more than what she comes to regard as the boredom of the strictly regulated routine of Anglo-India. Jhabvala's early portrait of Olivia paints a vivid picture of what life was like for a woman in an Anglo-Indian world that revolved around the duties of men. Even the language of the land is a strictly male preserve:

"Why? Mrs. Crawford speaks Hindustani; and Mrs. Minnies."
"Yes, but not with men. And they don't deliver deadly insults. It's a man's game, strictly."
"What isn't?" Olivia said. (*HAD*, 38–39)

Here too in this reference to Hindustani Jhabvala is pointing to a difference between (a) those who merge with India, first as administrators (rightly or wrongly) and later as seekers, and (b) those whose feelings for India never allow them peace in that country. Characters like Beth Crawford, who "spoke Urdu (the language of the Palace) if not well at any rate with confidence" (*HAD*, 29); Douglas, who "spoke Hindustani very fluently" (*HAD*, 36); and indeed most of the members of the Anglo-Indian community and even the narrator of the later story, who is attempting to learn Hindi—all are understood by the Indians to whom they speak. This may be because the Indians also understand why those people are in India, and in this regard such people are closer to Judy than to Esmond or Professor Hoch.

The boredom Olivia experiences at home make Khatm—which provides, initially at least, a contrast to her life in Satipur—appear attractive. In Khatm she finds much to entertain her, including of course, the

Nawab himself, and as she finds him increasingly entertaining, so she begins to find Douglas more and more stuffy.

Through these complex contrasts, between Khatm and Satipur and between the Nawab and Douglas, Jhabvala explores the question of East and West. The Nawab and Douglas each carries with him the invisible presence of an entire culture that has made him what he is. The apparently straightforward East-West contrast these characters seem to embody is already apparent or implied in the complex and beautifully handled presentation of the curious relationship between the Nawab and Harry. The difficulty of the choice facing Olivia, the continuous fascination of West with East, the difficulty of leaving, and the obsession with "otherness"— with the repressed power and sexuality of the climate, landscape, and culture of India, all embodied in the Nawab—are explored first through Harry.

While Olivia would like to be able to move freely between the two worlds, her pregnancy means that she must make a choice, and because she has already visited the Indian side of the East-West divide, her choice is rather limited. Ironically, the crude abortion she undergoes to prevent the Nawab from having his revenge on Douglas and the other Anglo-Indians (if, as he assumes, the child is black) is also a step toward the irreversible leap she takes when she flees to Khatm. Her decision to flee to the Nawab, away from Anglo-India, and also from England (which is where Adela Quested returned to) is an unusual decision for the time, and one that looks forward to the young questing figures of postindependence India whom Jhabvala writes about so well.

In the end Olivia appears to have surrendered to India, to the Nawab, in much the same way as 50 years later, the unnamed narrator, deliberately following in her footsteps, will surrender, and as Judy has surrendered too. These three characters stand apart from the other Western characters in *A Backward Place, A New Dominion,* and *Heat and Dust.* Ramlal Agarwal is thus only partly right when he suggests that the theme of the last three Indian novels is "[t]hat India overwhelms Westerners" (Agarwal 1990, 70). Etta and Clarissa, Evie and Margaret, and finally Lee too are overwhelmed by India; Judy, Olivia, and the unnamed narrator submit to India without being overwhelmed by it—they never lose the sense of their own identity, because they never reject their own backgrounds. The narrator of *Heat and Dust* is not ashamed of her British-Indian ancestry, and she describes her grandfather, Douglas Rivers, as "upright and just" (*HAD*, 1). Judy and the narrator of *Heat and Dust,* unlike other Europeans in Jhabvala's contemporary pictures of India, are self-effacing and frequently aware of the

Indian point of view, which other European characters are rarely prepared to try to understand.

If, as I have suggested, novels like *To Whom She Will* and *The Nature of
Passion* are novels of the first stage of the cycle Ruth Prawer Jhabvala
refers to in "Myself in India," and if her next three novels show Jhabvala
passing through the second stage and entering the third stage of the
cycle, her later Indian novels, particularly *A Backward Place* and *Heat and
Dust,* in which there are European characters at each of the three stages,
show that Jhabvala has indeed been "strapped to a wheel that goes round
and round" ("Myself in India," 9) through the cycle she describes. But
the novels that, like *Heat and Dust,* have more European characters in the
grip of the third stage are not simply anti-Indian novels; rather, they are
novels that, with remarkable honesty, portray both the good and the bad
aspects of India, as well as the effects the author has observed India to
have on Westerners who live there. Perhaps as the young Indian doctor in
Heat and Dust suggests, it is not a country where Western people should
live. Indeed, after the publication of *Heat and Dust* Jhabvala herself made
a new home in the United States, and her next two novels, which share
much in common thematically with her later Indian novels, are set
predominantly outside India.

Chapter Five
Sufferers, Seekers, and the Beast That Moves
The Short Stories

Ruth Prawer Jhabvala has published five volumes of short stories, the first four being *Like Birds, like Fishes* (1963), *A Stronger Climate* (1968), *An Experience of India* (1971), and *How I Became a Holy Mother* (1976). Many of the stories included in these four volumes were originally published in such magazines as the *New Yorker* (for whom Jhabvala wrote regularly), *Encounter, London Magazine,* and *Cornhill Magazine.* The fifth volume is a collection of stories selected by Jhabvala from the previous four, published under the title *Out of India*—a delicately ambiguous title that can be taken either as an indication that the stories draw on Jhabvala's 25 years in India or as a statement about the author herself, who now lives in New York.

The tales range from beautifully written character studies like "The Man with the Dog" to closely observed portraits of Indian life like "Sixth Child." While stories like the title story of the first collection, "Like Birds, like Fishes," are concerned with Indians, stories such as those in *A Stronger Climate* are concerned with Europeans living in India. Marriage, particularly the problem of mixed marriage, which is the subject of "The Aliens," is a common theme. Some tales, like "An Experience of India," are as complete as a novel, while others, like "Prostitutes," present short scenes, apparently plucked at random from everyday life, with no significant beginning or ending. These stories, in which nothing is resolved, appear to emphasize the timelessness of Indian life itself, in much the same way the presence of the punkah-wallah does in *A Passage to India.* The tone of the stories varies from satire and comedy in a piece like "The Award" to the moving, melancholy mood of "Desecration." While the majority are, like her first six novels, set in Delhi, others reach farther afield, to Bombay in "A Star and Two Girls" and other stories or to England in "A Course of English Studies," which is set in the Midlands, and "A Birthday in London," which stands apart from Jhabvala's other collected stories in that it is concerned neither with India nor with Indian characters. The stories also make use of different narrative voices, ranging from the first person (both male, as in "The Interview," and female, as in "My First Marriage") to various third-person perspectives, including the frequent omniscient narrator. Others, such as "Lekha" and "The Man with the Dog," combine a first-person narrative with a limited third-person portrait of the central character.

Thus in "Lekha," for instance, two distinct portraits are produced—that of the central character, Lekha, and that of the narrator, who reveals as much about herself as she does about Lekha. The social satire surrounding the descriptions of civil service parties recalls the satire of the early novels, and in particular that surrounding Chandra Prakesh and his wife in *The Nature of Passion*. While recalling the satire of earlier novels, though, "Lekha" also looks ahead, in its narrative technique, to later novels. As Yasmine Gooneratne explains, "It is Ruth Jhabvala's first attempt, and a highly successful one, at the indirect revelation of character that we have seen in more finished and sophisticated forms in *Heat and Dust* and AUTOBIOGRAPHY OF A PRINCESS. As in *Heat and Dust*, a female narrator relates the story of another woman's scandalous love-affair, unconsciously laying her own soul bare as she does so" (Gooneratne, 237).

While the stories stand by themselves, they also share some common ground with the novels. Marriage, as I noted, is important in a number of stories, and food is used in much the same way it is in Jhabvala's early novels. But of greater significance is Jhabvala's interest in European characters in India, an interest that becomes increasingly apparent in her novels and is reflected in her stories too.

Stories concerned with European characters appear in all Jhabvala's collections of stories, and in the second collection, *A Stronger Climate*, all nine stories involve Europeans in India. Divided thematically into two parts, *A Stronger Climate* looks at these Europeans as "seekers" and "sufferers." The seekers are all young people who have come to India in search of something, whether it be inner enlightenment, as in "A Spiritual Call"; information, as in "The Biographer"; or love (in one of its many manifestations), as in the other tales in this section. The sufferers, on the other hand, are all elderly Europeans who have stayed on after independence and are forced to live out their remaining days in India, stranded in the country just as they appear to be stranded forever in the third stage of Jhabvala's cycle of responses to India. The interest in seekers continues in *An Experience of India* and *How I Became a Holy Mother*, although these books are not exclusively concerned with Europeans. Three of the collections contain a story that focuses on a young woman on a spiritual quest, which is also the major theme of *A New Dominion* and *Heat and Dust*. The narrators of all these stories are well suited for Jhabvala's purposes—they are, as Laurie Sucher notes, "intelligent and unconventional" (Sucher, 40), which makes them ideal observers of all they see around them.

"A Spiritual Call" satirically portrays life in an ashram, as Daphne, a young English girl, follows her guru, Swamiji, to India after their initial meeting in London. Swamiji, who, not content with his simple community, wants to build "[a] tip-top, up-to-date ashram . . . with air-conditioned meditation cells and a central dining-hall" (*SC*, 99) and looks forward to his trip to America and the comforts of Mrs. Gay Fisher's California mansion complete with "swimming-pool and all amenities" (*SC*, 107), is critically portrayed. But it is not a vicious portrait like that of the swami in "An Experience of India." In "A Spiritual Call" Ruth Prawer Jhabvala makes perhaps her clearest statement about the importance of a sari as a symbol of the adoption of Indian values: Daphne is given a sari by Swamiji, to wear as the uniform of his disciples, a symbol to denote his ownership of her, as well as her acceptance of him.

Interestingly, Daphne's role as secretary to the swami in "A Spiritual Call" is repeated in Evie's role in *A New Dominion*, and the swamis of both the story and the novel are writing books; in addition, Ahmed's relationship with Henry's servant, Ramu, is similar to the relationship Jhabvala later develops between Gopi and Shyam. These similarities, however, are minor given that Lee's story in the novel parallels the story "An Experience of India" throughout. In fact "An Experience of India" is unusual among Jhabvala's stories in being an obvious example of a tale later used as the basis of a novel, namely *A New Dominion*.

In "An Experience in India," written in the first-person, the narrator admits she "had come to India to *be* in India. I wanted to be changed."[1] Like Lee's, her travels are unplanned, and both characters frequently accept the offers of hospitality they receive from fellow passengers on trains and buses. Moreover, after wandering for some time both characters embark on spiritual quests that lead them to an ashram and a guru.

But it is not only the character of Lee that owes much to the earlier story; the gurus are remarkably similar in both works. The one in the tale is particularly interested in the fact that Henry, the narrator's husband, is a journalist, while Swamiji in the novel is interested in Raymond because he is in the publishing business; in both cases the swami sees a way of spreading his word abroad. Jean, a young European woman in "An Experience in India," can likewise be seen as a forerunner of Evie in *A New Dominion*. Jean "was quite white, waxen, and her hair too was completely faded and colourless" (*HM*, 130), while Evie "was so pale and weak and blonde that she was almost invisible" (*ND*, 100). Both young women wear white cotton saris, and both are utterly humble and submissive before their gurus. Neither the narrator of the story nor Lee can easily adopt such attitudes.

The zenith of both story and novel are reached when the narrator and Lee, respectively, are raped by their gurus; however, while the rapes themselves are quite similar, the ways they are presented are quite different. The guru in "An Experience of India," though initially frightening, is effectively reduced to ridicule when he asks, "How many men have you slept with?" (*HM*, 133)—the same question that the many Indians the narrator has slept with on her travels have asked her. When he cries, "Bitch!" (*HM*, 133) as he lies on top of her, the horror is taken out of the situation, and she is able to laugh with relief as she realizes he is no different from the men she has met on her earlier travels. Swamiji in *A New Dominion*, however, remains a frightening and cruel figure, and there is no such relief for Lee.

Both the narrator of the story and Lee in the novel leave their ashrams, but fail to find any lasting happiness afterward, and when the opportunity to go home is offered, neither is able to accept it. The narrator somewhat naively decides to stay and resume her travels, while Lee knows that she will inevitably return to the ashram. *A New Dominion* owes a great deal to the earlier story, and it is interesting to see how Jhabvala's ideas have developed from story to novel—the novel presents a far bleaker picture and perhaps reflects Jhabvala's despair of ever reaching an understanding of India that isn't in some way naive. Thus it may be that the swami's cruelty is used to show how little a Western viewpoint is capable of comprehending the nature of India. Lee's rape, like the pseudorape of Adela Quested in *A Passage to India*, is perhaps an indication of the naïveté of everything Lee, like Adela, has been thinking about India up to that point. It is too easy for Lee, and the Western reader, to leap from one view of India to another, never understanding that no simple view is adequate. As Godbole explains in *A Passage to India*, the good and the bad are indeed indivisible.

Jhabvala's dissatisfaction with India is not, however, reflected in all her stories about gurus. "How I Became a Holy Mother," again a first-person narrative, gives an often-comic and altogether-more-tolerant portrait of an ashram, as signaled by the ironic tile. In this story the narrator is not destroyed and has no bad experiences. The guru is different from the earlier ones, even in his name: "this one was just called plain Master, in English" (*HM*, 139). Unlike the guru figures in earlier stories, Master has no longings to go abroad or to build a new ashram; he is happy to let his existing one grow as the need arises, and he is quite content with his present surroundings. As he explains to Katie, the narrator: "I stand in the middle of Times Square or Piccadilly, London, and I look up and there are all the beautiful beautiful buildings stretching so high up into heaven: yes I look at them but it is not them I see at all, Katie! Not them at all!" (*HM*, 144). What he sees in his mind's eye are the mountains and rivers surrounding the ashram, which reflect his own perfect happiness, as Katie and Vishwa (the swami's disciple who becomes the new spiritual leader) find when they begin to travel abroad and, like Master, miss the life of the ashram. The narrator's sexual experiences in the community are not the violent encounters of "An Experience of India," and as a result the story presents a more positive picture of an ashram.

I have discussed these three narratives at some length and in relation to the novel *A New Dominion* because while they all treat the same theme, their different approaches illustrate Jhabvala's ability to deal with a single subject in a variety of ways. The same is true of her treatment of marriage and of all the various topics she writes about in her stories.

In "A Birthday in London" Jhabvala describes life for a group of German Jews living in London. As noted in chapter 1, this is the clearest description in Jhabvala's fiction of the life she must have known as a child and young adult in England. Groups of exiled Europeans similar to the one gathered here for Sonia's birthday recur in Jhabvala's Indian stories, particularly in the stories drawn together under the heading "The Sufferers" in *A Stronger Climate*, and in the novel *A Backward Place*, too. Later, of course, Jhabvala takes up the lives of German or Polish Jews in New York in her uncollected stories "Commensurate Happiness"[2] and "Grandmother,"[3] and again in her ninth novel, *In Search of Love and Beauty*.

"Commensurate Happiness" is another clear example of a story prefiguring a novel. Many of the characters in the story have more fully developed parallels in *In Search of Love and Beauty* in particular and in *Three Continents* too. Jeannette, the widowed grandmother, is a forerunner of Louise Sonnenblick of *In Search of Love and Beauty*, while her

daughter Sandra is an earlier version of Louise's daughter Marietta. And
the relationship between the cousins Hughie and Marie in the story is
similar to the relationship between Mark and his adopted sister, Natasha,
in *In Search of Love and Beauty* (and to the relationship between the twins
Harriet and Michael Wishwell in *Three Continents*.) Wanda, also of
German descent, is clearly another Regi. Jeannette's apartment crowded
with inherited European furniture is seen once more in Louise's apartment; indeed, the whole family situation in the story is similar to that
which occurs in *In Search of Love and Beauty*.

At the heart of the ironically titled story "Commensurate Happiness"
lie Wanda's birthday parties (just as Regi's are important events in the
novel). The earliest birthday party recalled in the story is one held for
Wanda shortly before the death of Otto, Jeannette's husband. As what
amounts to a final request, Otto asks that Wanda, his mistress, celebrate
her birthday in his house, with his family: "So it happened that the first
time Wanda was allowed to enter their home was in honour of her own
birthday" ("Happiness," 8). This birthday party forces the other guests,
Jeannette and the young children, Hughie and Marie, to accept Otto's
mistress into their family. At a later birthday party, the centerpiece of the
story, Wanda takes it on herself to push the two cousins into marriage,
and after her intervention the reluctant Hughie does, in his own fashion,
propose to the eager Marie. The situation is, we learn, similar to that
which brought about the marriage between Jeannette and Otto. When
Jeannette remonstrates, Wanda justifies her actions: "That's the way it
has to be done: if young people don't know where they're going, the
family has to take over" ("Happiness," 10). And we are immediately told
that "As a matter of fact that's how it had been done with Jeannette and
Otto" ("Happiness," 10).

The happiness likely to be enjoyed by Hughie and Marie is commensurate to that enjoyed by Jeannette and Otto. As Jeannette had to endure
Otto's affairs, so Marie will have to suffer Hughie's homosexual relationships. Jeannette is willing to accept this state of affairs, not only for
herself, but for Marie too, when she supports the idea of a marriage that
only Hughie seems reluctant to seal: "He does care for you. He loves you.
As far as he can, he does. What more do you want?" she added—rather
impatiently, for it seemed to her that Marie was being unreasonable in
her expectations. She too would have to learn that one lived on earth and
not in heaven" ("Happiness," 11). Marie's so called unreasonable expectations are that her future husband should love her, and it is significant
that it is another woman, her own grandmother, who scorns the expec-

tations. The happiness Marie can expect is thus commensurate with the diminished expectations Jeannette pushes her toward, expectations that she, like Jeannette before her, is prepared to accept. In this story, in *In Search of Love and Beauty*, and in *Three Continents* Jhabvala appears to blame women who accept this course of events and by so doing help perpetuate the undervalued role women perceive for themselves in society. Such attitudes, clearly expressed in this story, suggest that Jhabvala may at times be quietly beating a feminist drum in her fiction.

In the stories "A Birthday in London" and "Commensurate Happiness" and in the novels *In Search of Love and Beauty* and *Three Continents* birthdays are important. Certainly the stories and novels celebrating birthdays are the fictions that seem closest to the author's own family circumstances. (Of course, the celebration of birthdays is very important in German culture, much more than in English culture.)

The Sufferers of the three stories "An Indian Citizen," "Miss Sahib," and "The Man with the Dog"—Dr. Ernst, Miss Tuhy, and Boekelman, respectively—are all elderly Europeans who have stayed on in India too long. Like Lucy in Paul Scott's *Staying On* (1977), they are "alone . . . amid the alien corn, waking, sleeping, alone for ever and ever."[4] Like Scott's treatment of Tusker and Lucy Smalley, Jhabvala's treatment of these elderly "sufferers" is tender and sympathetic, yet penetrating too. It is stories like these, along with tales like "The Aliens" and "The Young Couple," both of which portray an Englishwoman married to an Indian husband, that reflect Jhabvala's own experiences of India and her own feelings of expatriation and alienation.

There is gentle irony in "An Indian Citizen" and "Miss Sahib," wherein the two central characters attempt to adopt India and to belong in a way vaguely reminiscent of the young seekers of the stories in the first section of *A Stronger Climate*. Indeed, Dr. Ernst, even though he may be an Indian citizen, remains painfully an outsider. His insistence that he has a great many Indian friends is comically undermined when he visits the dreadful Miss Chawla and even attempts to put a brave interpretation on her obvious rudeness and displeasure at seeing him: "It was foolish, he told himself, to feel hurt or slighted. She had not meant anything personal. . . . It was kind enough of her to have let him stay as long as she did. She was his good friend and esteemed and liked him as much as he did her" (*SC*, 154). Contrary to "looking for offence where none was meant" (*SC*, 154), as he persuades himself he is doing, Dr. Ernst is refusing to see offense where it is clearly given, turning a proverbial blind eye to what he does not want to—and cannot, if his position in India is to remain tolerable—allow himself to believe. His unfortunate position in India is cushioned, as is Etta's, by the existence of a circle of European friends that he can always turn to for comfort—literally, in the case of Maiska's flat, with its comfortable armchairs, Mozart records, and good strong coffee. Only here, in a European environment, can he truly relax and feel at home.

Miss Tuhy in "Miss Sahib" has no such haven to turn to when her experience of India turns sour. Like Dr. Ernst, Miss Tuhy believes India is her true home and Indians her true friends. The story traces her disillusionment with India and with her Indian friends, and draws to a conclusion that sees the sad, pathetic figure of the elderly Englishwoman realizing that she does miss England, and does want to go home, but aware too that "she no longer had the fare home to England, not even on the cheapest route" (*SC*, 181).

The narrator of "The Man with the Dog" records quite clearly the reasons she (and Jhabvala) sees for elderly Europeans like Boekelman being in India, as she meditates on his friends:

> They have all of them been in India for many, many years—twenty-five, thirty—but I know they would much rather be somewhere else. They only stay here because they feel too old to go anywhere else and start a new life. They came here for different reasons—some because they were married to Indians, some to do business, others as refugees and because they couldn't get a visa for anywhere else. None of them has ever tried to learn any Hindi or to get to know anything about our India. They have some Indian "friends," but these are all very rich and important people—like maharinis and cabinet ministers, they don't trouble with ordinary people at all. But really they are only friends with one another, and they always like each other's company best. (*SC*, 193)

In this story Jhabvala controls her first-person narrative beautifully to present a third-person portrait of Boekelman, a sad, helpless old man who has stayed in India too long, and combines it with a contrasting first-person portrait of the narrator that shows the great happiness she derives from this old man, quite contrary to the expected behavior of an Indian widow.

Jhabvala treats the subject of a would-be sufferer very differently in "The Englishwoman," a story included in the American edition of *How I Became a Holy Mother* but omitted from the British one. It is the story of an Englishwoman, Sadie, who at age 52 and after 30 years of married life in India, decides to leave her adopted country and return "home" to

England. This decision results from Sadie's taking stock of her life in a way that Jhabvala's sufferers rarely manage to do. And without over-stressing the autobiographical element of this story, it appears to reflect Jhabvala's own need to return to the West after a quarter-century in India. Indeed, Sadie's explanation to her daughter "that when people get older they begin to get very homesick for the place in which they were born and grew up and that this homesickness becomes worse and worse till in the end life becomes almost unbearable."[5] echoes Jhabvala's explanation of her own desire to leave India in such pieces as "Disinher-itance," her Neil Gunn Memorial Lecture, in which she refers to "a terrible hunger of homesickness that I cannot describe it was so terrible, so consuming" ("Disinheritance," 11).

Sadie can trace her decision to leave to a particular day 20 years earlier when her son Dev was ill. She contrasts the child's stifling sickroom, crowded with female relatives paying attention of various sorts to the patient, with her own childhood sickbeds, wherein the quiet and bore-dom were interrupted only by her mother bringing in her medicine. These images of the two sickrooms effectively define the differences between the two countries in Sadie's mind and lead to her realization that she is not Indian, can never become Indian, and, perhaps more signifi-cantly, has no desire to become Indian.

Sadie's inability to become Indian and the strength of her desire to return to England are melliflously evoked in the closing sentences of the story. There the moonlit Indian scene in her garden is transformed into the memory-lit landscape of the English downs, fresh, cold, wet, and with a freedom in the wind the strength of which Sadie has never felt in India. It is a wonderful image, and one that underlines perfectly Jhab-vala's interest in place and belonging, an interest in inheritance that is perhaps best understood by the disinherited—by characters like Sadie or by Jhabvala herself.

The stories concerned solely with Indian characters, like the early novels, demonstrate Jhabvala's delight in India and show that she is indeed an "outsider with unusual insight" (Agarwal 1973, 11). "The Widow" illustrates this position well. In this story Durga has refused to accept the traditional role of widow—"the cursed one who had commit-ted the sin of outliving her husband and was consequently to be num-bered among the outcasts"[6]—and has refused to be condemned "to that perpetual mourning, perpetual expiation, which was the proper lot of widows" (*LBLF*, 58) and is the wish of some of her more orthodox relatives.

Durga's life has been one of emptiness, in her marriage to an old and impotent man and now in widowhood, and in a quest for satisfaction— or, more particularly, sexual satisfaction—Durga first turns to dreams of the god Krishna and, when this fails to fill the void inside her, then turns her attention to Govind, the son of her tenants. Durga is drawn to Govind not only by her unfulfilled maternal feelings, but also by her unsatisfied sexual desires: "His teeth were large and white, his hair sprang from a point on his forehead. Everything about him was young and fresh and strong—even his smell, which was that of a young animal full of sap and sperm" (*LBLF*, 69). Durga's feelings for Govind, which she demonstrates through gifts of money and promises of more presents, are, like her earlier passion for Krishna, destined to remain unrequited. When this passion too ends in disappointment for Durga, after she surrenders to her passion for Govind and is repelled, she is finally defeated and prepared to give in to her relatives and the traditional role of a widow.

In her portrayal of Durga's widowhood and in her depiction of the scheming of both Durga's relatives and her tenants, the Puris, Jhabvala demonstrates just how well she had observed life in an Indian joint family.

The irony present in her early novels is evident in the close of this story, where the scheming of the relatives and Durga's breakdown are justified in the final paragraph:

> The relatives were glad that Durga had at last come round and accepted her lot as a widow. They were glad for her sake. There was no other way for widows but to lead humble, bare lives; it was for their own good. For if they were allowed to feed themselves on the pleasures of the world, then they fed their own passions too, and that which should have died in them with the deaths of their husbands would fester and boil and overflow into sinful channels. Oh yes, said the relatives, wise and knowing, nodding their heads, our ancestors knew what they [were] doing when they laid down these rigid rules for widows; and though nowadays perhaps, in these modern times, one could be a little more lenient— for instance, no one insisted that Durga should shave her head—still, on the whole, the closer one followed the old traditions, the safer and the better it was. (*LBLF*, 78)

This paragraph is interesting for it shows that Jhabvala is sensitive to the traditional status of widows and the way in which they were seen by their relatives, yet the very reasons concealed behind that traditional view are what Jhabvala is subverting in this ironic story. In this masterful paragraph she subtly questions the motives of Durga's relatives; when she writes, "it was for their own good," she is, of course, referring to the good of widows, but in the context of this story she could also be referring to Durga's relatives. And similarly, the closing line of the story leaves up in the air the question, Better for whom?

The most disturbing of all Jhabvala's stories is "Desecration," which draws to a close her fourth collection, *How I Became a Holy Mother.* This tale, told very deliberately in a third-person voice, though clearly from Sofia's point of view, relates the story of a young Muslim girl who is married to Raja Sahib, an elderly Hindu landowner who always treats her with great kindness. Sofia's disaffection with her life has similarities with the sense of constraint Olivia Rivers feels in the Anglo-Indian world of *Heat and Dust.* In a search for fulfillment Sofia has an affair with the superintendent of police, Bakhtawar Singh, and is drawn down into a state of emotional turmoil that causes her to commit suicide in the hotel room in which she had been meeting her lover.

In one sense the story of the affair is archetypal: the sensitive, educated woman who by marriage at least belongs to a higher class is drawn into a sordid affair with a brutal, uneducated man from a lower class. Her quest for passion and sexual fulfillment causes Sofia to become reckless; to be talked about by everyone in the village as her affair becomes widely known; and masochistically to pursue Bakhtawar Singh and submit to him in an act of sexual union that gives the story both its apogee and its title. When Bakhtawar Singh hears an old man saying the Muhammadan prayers in the next room, he urges Sofia to pray too:

She knelt naked on the floor and began to pray the way the old man was praying in the next room, knocking her forehead on the ground. Bakhtawar Singh urged her on, watching her with tremendous pleasure from the bed. Somehow the words came back to her and she said them in chorus with the old man next door. After a while, Bakhtawar Singh got off the bed and joined her on the floor and mounted her from behind. He wouldn't let her stop praying, though. "Go on," he said, and how he laughed as she went on. Never had he had such enjoyment out of her as on that day. (*HM*, 266)

But even this act of gross violation is not enough to cool Sofia's passion; rather, she still attempts to persuade him to meet her more often. Nor is her passion cooled by the voices of the village, which are discussing her behind her back. Only when she reads out the drama her husband has just written for her and comes across the line "Oh, if thou didst but know what it is like to live in hell the way I do!" (*HM*, 268) does her position become clear to her. Her husband's hell is both the pain of an unexplained illness and the pain of the love he feels for Sofia, while her hell is the hell she suffers as a result of her longing for Bakhtawar Singh, a longing that causes her heart to physically ache like a disease that "would get worse and pass through many stages before it was finished with her" (*HM*, 267). It is a hell made worse by the look the Raja Sahib gives her: "There had never been anyone in the world who looked into her eyes the way he did, with such love but at the same time with a tender respect that would not reach farther into her than was permissible between two human beings" (*HM*, 268). This is a respect Bakhtawar Singh does not give her; rather, the act of desecration he commits while she prays is the embodiment of the desecration he has committed by violating her as a human being.

Unlike Jhabvala's other stories, there are no deft touches of comedy in this story, no subtle ironic nuances to relieve the tragedy of the story, and nothing to diminish its power.

Ruth Prawer Jhabvala's vision of India as presented in her short stories appears to be influenced, even controlled, by the cycle she describes in her important essay "Myself in India." In "An Experience of India," the title story of the volume in which her revealing essay appeared as an introduction, the narrator passes through all three stages of the cycle Jhabvala describes in "Myself in India." As the story ends, the cycle can be seen to be renewing itself as India reasserts its hold over the narrator; she, like Jhabvala, is "strapped to a wheel" ("Myself in India," 9) that will control her responses to India. The Indian beast is an animal that appears to stop thrashing beneath Ruth Prawer Jhabvala only when she leaves India and moves to New York.

Chapter Six
Under a Different Sky
The American Novels

In Ruth Prawer Jhabvala's story "The Englishwoman," Sadie, the Englishwoman of the title, feels an overwhelming homesickness after 30 years in India and decides to leave her family and return to England. For Jhabvala, though, unlike Sadie, the option of returning home was not there. The events that overtook Europe in the 1930s and 1940s meant that the Germany of her childhood no longer existed; however, she was able to return to her roots, at least to a degree, by moving to New York. As she explains about an earlier visit to that city, "I met the people who should have remained in my life—people I went to school with in Cologne, with exactly the same background as my own, same heritage, same parentage. . . . The accent of the tongue may be American but the accent of the soul has retained the intonation of the European past" ("Disinheritance," 12–13).

In Search of Love and Beauty (1983) and *Three Continents*, (1987) mark a significant departure for Jhabvala, whom many critics have seen as a writer who interprets India for Western readers.[1] In both these novels Jhabvala attempts to combine her triple European, Indian, and American heritage. The characters who populate *In Search of Love and Beauty* are mostly Westerners, though two Indians, Ahmed and Sujata, have minor roles. Moreover, for the first time in her fiction Jhabvala returns to the German childhood she knew but rarely writes about. In her Neil Gunn Memorial Lecture of 1979 she acknowledges her reluctance to write about this period of her life: "the early happy German-Jewish bourgeois family years—1927 to 1933—they should be that profound well of memory and experience (childhood and ancestral) from which as a writer I should have drawn. I never have. I've never written about those years. To tell you the truth, until today I've never even mentioned them" ("Disinheritance," 6). Perhaps it is only as a resident of New York, whereby she has returned, at least in a symbolic way, to her German-Jewish roots by joining the thousands of other Jewish refugees who

flocked to New York in the 1930s and 1940s, that she feels ready to
return to that dormant part of her past.

In exploring the heritage of her German-Jewish protagonists Jhabvala
also explores aspects of the heritage of her adopted country, the heritage
of the Hudson River Valley (which features in both *In Search of Love and
Beauty* and *Three Continents*) that is at the very heart of America's cultural
heritage. Laurie Sucher has thoroughly discussed the Greco-Roman
mythological allusions that pervade *In Search of Love and Beauty*, even
from the opening page, where Leo Kellerman is introduced as "An
Adonis! . . . An Apollo!—A god."[2] Jennifer Livett, in an essay entitled "Propinquity and Distance: The America of Jhabvala and Bellow,"[3]
examines Jhabvala's exploration of American cultural heritage in both *In
Search of Love and Beauty* and *Three Continents*. Both critics provide useful
insights into these novels and help illustrate the tremendous depth to be
found in Jhabvala's fiction, particularly in the richly textured *In Search of
Love and Beauty*.

In contrast to the approaches taken by Sucher and Livett, however, I
want to concentrate in this chapter on the themes linking these two
novels to the Indian novels and stories discussed in the preceding
chapters, to show that they are an essential part of Jhabvala's fictional
oeuvre, one marking a development that is entirely consistent with the
course of her other fiction. Indeed, in an interview with Anna Rutherford
and Kirsten Holst Peterson shortly after the publication of *Heat and Dust*
Jhabvala foreshadows such a development: "Having assimilated all this
Indian experience I don't want to forget it or cast it off; what I want to do
is to take it out again as a Westerner, enriched by what I have learnt
there. . . . I can't throw away the past twenty-four years nor do I want
to" (Rutherford and Peterson, 377). And in another interview not long
after this Jhabvala speaks more specifically about her future aims as a
writer: "Something I would like to do is combine my three backgrounds:
my European background because it was Continental; and then I had an
English education. Then I had a 25-year immersion into India and now
I am beginning an immersion into America. So if I can bring all these
elements together, well, that's just fine by me" (Mooney, 52). In both *In
Search of Love and Beauty* and *Three Continents* Jhabvala does successfully
combine these elements. In *In Search of Love and Beauty* her focus on
German-Jewish refugees brings the presence of both Europe and America into her fiction, and through Marietta, who resembles the seekers of
the later Indian novels, the presence of India enters the pages of the novel
too. In *Three Continents* Jhabvala's desire to combine her three back-

grounds is even more clearly fulfilled. The novel is divided into three sections, one set in America, one in England, and one in India.

The title of Jhabvala's first American novel, *In Search of Love and Beauty*, links it inextricably with her Indian novels. As Laurie Sucher explains, "Every protagonist in Jhabvala's fiction has been 'in search of love and beauty.' . . . This novel, whose slightly ironic title contains the essential Jhabvala theme, examines the effects of this search on a group of German and Austrian refugees in New York, and two generations of their descendents" (Sucher, 168). Jhabvala's interest in guru figures, first evident in *The Householder*,[4] continues in the form of the charismatic Leo Kellerman of *In Search of Love and Beauty* and in the figure of the Rawul of *Three Continents*. Like her Indian fiction, these novels are concerned with religious exploiters, and also with political ones, and of course with the victims of both. The Western seekers who populate her Indian fiction are here found in Leo's followers and in the Rawul's devotees. Jhabvala's interest in human relationships and how characters behave in particular situations is always at the root of her Indian novels—despite opinions to the contrary, Jhabvala's novels are far more than an introduction to India for Western readers—and it is also at the root of her American ones.

In *In Search of Love and Beauty* the search for love and beauty is closely linked to a search for identity or heritage. Jhabvala's interest in her German heritage is also evident in intertextual references that occur in *In Search of Love and Beauty*, especially in the reference to Goethe's domestic epic *Hermann und Dorothea* (which, significantly, appears early in the novel), the book that Louise's long-suffering and patient-to-a-fault husband, Bruno, is reading at one point in the novel. As Laurie Sucher elucidates, the plot of *Hermann und Dorothea* is paralleled in the situation of Bruno and Louise: "Like *In Search of Love and Beauty* itself, Goethe's epic concerns refugees, an engagement, and parents' relations with their children. It celebrates the beauties of the Rhine Valley—very much like the Hudson valley. The Hermann of the title is a reserved, modest young man who falls in love with heroic, beautiful and large Dorothea. In this the pair are reminiscent of modest Bruno and heroic Louise" (Sucher, 181). Given Jhabvala's intertextual uses of E. M. Forster's *A Passage to India* and *The Hill of Devi*, in *A New Dominion* and *Heat and Dust* particularly, the parallel with Goethe's epic poem is certain to have been carefully considered. By introducing the title of Bruno's book Jhabvala in her own way is writing back to her German heritage, just as she had earlier written back to her English literary heritage.

The many Europeans in this novel who have lost their German, Austrian, or Jewish heritage in their forced migration from the lands of their births attempt to recapture it in the wonderfully evocative café the Old Vienna, with all its grandeur of a lost Europe, and through the cakes they buy at Blauberg's to celebrate various anniversaries. This search for a lost heritage is closely tied to the search for love and beauty that gives the book its title. Louise's grandson Mark, who has lost his heritage, in this case his father's family home in the Hudson River Valley, seeks to regain it by buying the Van Kuypen house and restoring it to its former period glory. By installing his lover, Kent, in the house, however, his search for his heritage becomes linked to his own search for love and beauty. Both Louise and her daughter Marietta (Mark's mother) also search for love and beauty. For Louise it is a search that leads to Leo and to another house in the Hudson River Valley; for Marietta it involves a succession of lovers, including Leo, and an involvement with India. Ironically, Natasha, Mark's adopted sister, a quintessential Jewish orphan, is the only character who *has* truly lost her heritage (even Louise and Bruno are surrounded by family furniture, brought with them from Germany, in their New York apartment, and the Old Vienna and Blauberg's are part of their transported heritage too). Yet Natasha is also the only one who is not searching for anything, who is content with what she has and who she is.[5] This quality is particularly evident when Natasha is staying at Leo's Academy: "While everyone else in the Academy was busy looking into themselves, Natasha spent long hours looking out of the attic window" (*SLB*, 140). This ability to look out of a window and see beauty in the sky or in the landscape is a clear indication that a Jhabvala character is content and fulfilled.

Regi's "circle of women friends—all, like herself and Louise, German or Austrian refugees" who gather in her "smart Park Avenue apartment" (*SLB*, 5) to meet Leo are at the same time reminiscent of both the sufferers and the seekers of Jhabvala's short stories. Like the groups of Westerners in Delhi who gather at the Hochstadts' comfortable flat, or the circle of friends, including Dr. Ernst, who seek refuge in the European atmosphere of Maiska's flat in "An Indian Citizen," Regi's friends are drawn together by their sense that they, like Dr. Ernst and his friends, are stranded in a foreign land; they cannot return home, not because they lack the financial means, as is the case with Dr. Ernst and with Miss Tuhy in "Miss Sahib," but because home, prewar Germany, is no longer there. Louise, Regi, and their cohorts also have much in common with the seekers of those earlier stories. Whereas the young

Western women of the Indian stories are drawn to the mostly unholy gurus of the Indian landscape, Louise, Regi and their friends (again mostly women) are attracted to the charms of the apparent charlatan Leo Kellerman. Regi, of course, soon tires of Leo and is scornful of Louise's relationship with him and her continuing, albeit passive, support for his ideas.

In fact, Regi has much in common with an earlier Jhabvala character—Etta of *A Backward Place*. In that novel Etta makes a scene in a restaurant where she is having coffee with Clarissa:

> Etta took a sip from her coffee and then beckoned to the waiter: "I asked for coffee." He stared at her. "This isn't coffee," said Etta. "It's yesterday's gravy." He went on staring in incomprehension and she said wearily, "The man is stupid. Call the manager."
> "I don't know why you must always fuss so," Clarissa said. "I've drunk two cups of it and it's quite all right." (*BP*, 17–18)

In *In Search of Love and Beauty* a similar scene occurs in the beach hotel where Regi and Louise are staying on vacation in the Hamptons: "Regi didn't like it, she grumbled all the time, right from breakfast on when she sent back the coffee for not being strong enough, or found what she suspected was a spot of jam on the tablecloth. When Louise protested at the fuss she made, Regi said, 'They're charging enough, aren't they, my goodness'" (*SLB*, 93). Good strong coffee is frequently a symbol of a lost Europe in Jhabvala's fiction—for the sufferers marooned in India, as well as for the European refugees living in North America. And like Etta, Regi prefers to keep her blinds down to shut the light out of her apartment (*SLB*, 144). Similar types and themes appear in the Indian novels and stories, and they continue to recur in the American ones. As Jhabvala explains of the way she writes; "The same types come out again and again, I use one character and split that character up. I have certain leading figures in my life and I seem to use them again and again, presenting different facets of their personality so one person can play the role of fifty" (Rutherford and Peterson, 375).

This splitting-up of character can be seen in Marietta. Her initial enthusiasm for everything Indian resembles the early, naive enthusiasm of so many of Jhabvala's characters for everything Indian. Later when her attitudes change and she prefers to travel alone, "making no attempt to merge with people and landscape" (*SLB*, 24), she is like Raymond of *A New Dominion*, who finally prefers to see India from the detached position of a tourist. Still later, though, Marietta's attitude toward India changes once again when she is scratched on the hand by a kite (always a negative image in Jhabvala's fiction). The hysterical scene she makes and her subsequent irrational dislike of Indians show she has arrived at the third stage of the cycle Jhabvala suggests all Westerners in India pass through, a cycle that, because its various stages are included in the character of Marietta, Jhabvala still believes in.

Many other links exist between characters in this novel and those in the Indian novels: Leo Kellerman obviously resembles the many guru figures that populate the Indian novels and stories, in particular Swamiji of *A New Dominion*; Louise's unsuccessful attempts to be rid of Leo remind us of the many seekers who fruitlessly attempt to leave or forget their gurus; and so on.

Jhabvala, of course, is by no means simply rewriting earlier novels in a different geographic setting. Yet that she has changed the location of her fiction inevitably changes the way we as Western readers (and the way Indian readers too, though for different reasons) read and respond to her work. Because this novel is set in New York rather than India, the sense of an exotic "other" is presented in a new way. In the Indian novels and stories the Western sufferers and seekers were themselves slightly exotic by virtue of the fact that they were domiciled in or traveling through India; in *In Search of Love and Beauty* the sufferers and seekers appear more ordinary and are perhaps more accessible to many Western readers. In *In Search of Love and Beauty* Jhabvala deftly gives the sense of a number of overlapping cultural circles, age-group circles, professional circles—all operating simultaneously like a kind of palimpest, with each group being in some sense "other" to the rest but with certain individuals being able to pass from group to group with no apparent difficulty in the transition. In this regard *In Search of Love and Beauty* is by far the most socially complex, sophisticated, and revealing of all Jhabvala's novels.

In her last two Indian novels Jhabvala's narrative techniques changed, and the influence of her film work could clearly be seen in her novels. These techniques are further refined in *In Search of Love and Beauty*. *A New Dominion* is episodic, full of short scenes but nevertheless a chronological narrative. *Heat and Dust* switches frequently between two time periods 50 years apart, but each of these narratives adheres to a basic chronological progress, and the shifts between the two parallel stories do nothing to inhibit the chronology of the narrative. *In Search of Love and Beauty*, however, which spans some 60 years (including the flashbacks to Louise's childhood in D——in Germany), does not follow the ordered narrative structure of Jhabvala's earlier fiction; it instead shifts frequently from one period of Louise's life to another without warning, and in defiance of chronology.

As a result, we learn a great deal about Louise's family over three generations, and we learn very quickly, as the information is presented rapidly, without any narrative transitions between time periods. Jhabvala's work with film and her ability to adapt the techniques she has learned from writing for the cinema have allowed her to present what amounts to a compressed narrative. The information we receive about earlier time periods, apparently at random, does appear to mirror the way the mind recalls images and scenes from the past.

Jhabvala has taken great care with the presentation of the past in this novel. As historical figures and events appear in some of her Indian novels, so real historical figures—Max Reinhardt, Sigmund Freud, Wilhelm Reich—are named in this one: " 'And—eh—Leo—didn't you say you were with Reinhardt for a while?' 'Only two years.' 'And that poem you published in *Querschnitt?*' 'Not exactly a poem, more a play. A play in verse.' 'You must tell us about Freud. Can you believe it—he actually *met Freud?*' 'Long ago. Before Reich. After Reich, well—' He shrugged, disposing of Freud" (*SLB*, 6). The early references to these historical figures and to the literary arts journal *Querschnitt* (published in Berlin between 1921 and 1936) give Leo a certain amount of kudos with the friends gathered in Regi's apartment. The references to these figures also give us some idea of the types of beliefs Leo is likely to expound—encompassing the dramatic as well as the psychoanalytic and sexually oriented. Sucher also suggests that the character of Leo "contains satiric elements of the popular psychologist Fritz Perls, founder of the Esalen Institute in California, and the Russian mystic Gurdjieff" (Sucher, 172), and there are bound to be many other historical figures Jhabvala borrows from in her portrayal of Leo Kellerman. His academy is another version of the Indian ashrams that appeared in the Indian novels, and Leo's movement is reminiscent of the Indian religious groups the seekers of Jhabvala's Indian novels are attracted to, as well as being typical of the type of psychospiritual groups that grew up on the West Coast of North America in the 1960s. Similarly, the Rawul's Sixth World movement, while bearing some resemblance to the Bhagwan Sri Rajneesh movement, is also typical of the many such groups which have appeared in the writer's earlier fiction.

In *Three Continents* it is Michael Wishwell's search for love and beauty,

his expectation "of Beauty, Truth, and Justice,"[6] that brings him into
contact with the Rawul's movement and leads to the introduction of the
Rawul and his followers into Propinquity, the twins' family home in the
Hudson River Valley.

Crishi's interest in Michael is sparked by his discovery, after their
chance meeting in London, that Michael was staying at the U.S. embassy:
"Crishi got it out of him . . . that the ambassador was a family friend,
and after that everything else about our family; so then Crishi became
cordial in a different way, and he invited Michael to come and visit him;
and that was how Michael got involved with them all—that is, with the
Rawul and Rani and their entourage, and with their Sixth World
movement" (TC, 19). Crishi is interested in Michael for his family's
wealth, connections, and heritage. Yet at the outset of the novel Michael
has no interest in his family's heritage—unlike Mark of In Search of Love
and Beauty, who spends much of his time and money attempting to
recover his paternal American heritage. Etta of A Backward Place, we
might recall, also suffers as a result of, among other things, her lost
heritage and consequent sense of displacement in India. But as Propinquity (meaning "nearness in place or in blood relationship"), the title of
this section of the novel and the name of the Wishwell home, suggest,
heritage is important. The Rawul is very much aware of this idea; as
Harriet soon informs the reader, the Rawul particularly values the
heritage that Michael opens up to him: "what he especially valued in
using our house as his headquarters was that it placed him right at the
heart of American society" (TC, 45). That is, it gave him a sense of
belonging and thus effectively opened a significant door for the Rawul's
movement. And the Rawul makes much of his own heritage: "he had a
kingdom—a very small but very ancient one: the Kingdom of Dhoka"
(TC, 12–13). The kingdom may never have been of anything but minor
importance, but the Rawul emphasizes that it is an ancient one, that his
kingdom has a long heritage (he even claims for himself descent from the
moon). Yet we know too that the Rawul is no longer sanctioned to use
the title Rawul, that this has been taken away from him by the Indian
government. Thus to a degree the Rawul has lost his heritage; he is a
displaced/dispossessed person, which makes the heritage he can claim
and perhaps inherit from Michael and Harriet all the more appealing.

Even more significant is Crishi's and Rani's lack of any clear heritage.
Although we don't discover the full details of their backgrounds for some
time—because neither has a family heritage of which he or she can
boast—we do learn early in the novel that both have ambiguous back-

grounds, a point that stands out in a book that places so much emphasis on heritage. Only after Anna Sultan has written her article about the Rawul's movement does Harriet find out about Rani's background and learn the "truth," or at least a more convincing version, of Crishi's background. Both are of mixed parentage: "The Rani's mother, part-French and part-German, had married an Afghan" (*TC*, 138), while Crishi's mother, who we are told now lives in Hong Kong with a Chinese wrestler, is "partly Assamese, partly English—grew up in Calcutta and still has such a sweet Calcutta accent" (*TC*, 188). She isn't sure who Crishi's father is. Both Crishi and Rani, or Renée, as she is properly called, grew up in Europe, and both married early and had children. And given that so much store in *Three Continents* is placed on family heritage, the fact that neither Crishi nor Rani cares for his or her family is an implied condemnation.

The Rawul, Renée, and Crishi claim to be a family. It transpires, however, that Crishi, far from being the adopted son of the Rawul and his "wife" Renée, is in fact the lover of Renée, his "mother." Far from being a "family," then, this trio strikes a blow at the very structure of the family. These are the people—clearly caring nothing about family or propinquity—who invade Propinquity.

A sense of irony exists in the naming of Propinquity. Through the Wishwells Jhabvala makes it clear that the American family is already in decay when the Rawul and his entourage arrive on the scene: Michael's and Harriet's parents, Manton and Lindsay, are divorced; Manton's lover, Barbara, later to be his wife, is young enough to be his daughter; Lindsay is now involved in a long-term lesbian relationship with Jean; and even the twins' grandfather, Manton's father, had while his first wife was still alive run a ménage à trois that included his lover, later his second wife, Sonya.[7] Thus Jhabvala is suggesting that the American family and the whole notion of heritage are ripe for the plucking when Crishi, Renée, and the idealistic Rawul arrive in the midst of America's cultural heartland.

They arrive very much in the role of colonizers (and in this respect Jhabvala neatly reverses the usual Western-colonization-of-the-East motif), both spiritually, which is how the idealistic Michael sees them, and rather more literally, as appropriators of America's heritage. This aspect is nowhere more evident than in the Fourth of July celebrations that take place at Propinquity. Barbara and Jean, who from the beginning object to the presence of the Rawul and his followers at Propinquity, are outraged by the Rawul's intention to hoist the American flag. They see the action as an attempt to colonize or appropriate American heritage, to take away the celebrations from the Americans present. And indeed the Rawul hoists his own Sixth World flag alongside the Stars and Stripes, and the ceremony, conducted by the Rawul, is accompanied by his own anthem rather than "The Star Spangled Banner," the American national anthem. Following the flag-raising ceremony the colonizing continues when Crishi organizes a series of traditional games, including three-legged races. Crishi binds himself to Harriet "with a frayed fraternity necktie that had probably belonged to Lindsay's father" (*TC*, 59), a pun on the phrase "ties that bind" that combines, as Jennifer Livett has rightly pointed out, a suggestion of "the oldest tie of all, sex and marriage, with hints of the 'old tie' wealth and influence which precisely make [Harriet] of interest to this predator" (Livett, 70).

The colonization is further emphasized as first the local people are excluded from the grounds of Propinquity and later the house on the island is occupied by the movement's followers soon after the death of the twins' grandfather. It is also on the island, actually in the empty swimming pool at the nearby Linton house (and here there are distinct echoes of the Linton house in Emily Brontë's *Wuthering Heights*), that Crishi takes possession of Harriet physically. He is capable of exciting a sexual desire in Harriet that virtually enslaves her to him. Here, with the Eastern man enslaving the Western woman, is a neat reversal of the master-slave relationship of colonialism, which recalls the images of rape frequently used in Anglo-Indian fiction (in Paul Scott's *Raj Quartet*, for example) to depict the imperial yoke. Harriet's obsession may be slightly farfetched, but symbolically it serves a very useful purpose.

When Crishi and Harriet are married, one phase of the colonization is complete. As with the Fourth of July celebrations, the marriage (after the brief official ceremony at city hall) is performed in a symbolic ceremony of the Rawul's own devising, which in this instance takes place in Sonya's house, previously Harriet's grandfather's. The wedding can thus be seen as another example of the usurpers or invaders colonizing a bit more heritage, and it reflects the colonization of Harriet by Crishi. Ironically, the Rawul sees the wedding as a symbolic synthesis of East and West, whereas it is, rather, a symbolic colonization of West by East. And this sense of possession is evident much later in the novel, when Michael is beginning to doubt the validity of his (and Harriet's) involvement with the Rawul, Crishi, and the whole movement. At this point the Bari Rani, in tones of mock-maternal feeling, reminds Harriet, "you're ours; our child; just as much as the girls, you *belong* to us" (*TC*, 313; emphasis added). This is entirely the wrong interpretation of *propinquity*. Rather than suggesting a strong sense of familial feeling, the Bari Rani's words suggest ownership and the type of control that Swamiji of *A New Dominion* wished to exert over his followers.

Far from seeing Harriet as a cherished member of the family, Crishi and Renée (who first proposes their marriage) have an eye on Harriet's money, as does the Rawul. That Crishi, like the usurpers of Jane Austen's novels, is nothing more than a fortune hunter is made plain at various stages of the novel. In England, for example, the Bari Rani tells Harriet, "You're exactly the sort of innocent person they would trap. Trap and use" (*TC*, 171). By "they" the Bari Rani means Crishi and Renée, but her words could apply to the Rawul too. Further confirmation of his own aims comes from Crishi himself. He candidly admits to Harriet his desire for wealth: "I wouldn't have married you without it—without the money—I'd have wanted to but it wouldn't have worked out" (*TC*, 225). Harriet, gullible as ever, believes Crishi needs her money for the movement, even though Crishi, more explicit than usual about his craving for riches, tells her that "he needed money for the movement—but also for himself; because it was so unbearable not to have it" (*TC*, 225). And Crishi admits that the same is true of Renée. Indeed, we have already seen the result of an earlier invasion, in Renée's successful colonization of Rupert and in the appropriation of his wealth. Rupert is left without a family home, poor, and finally imprisoned as a result of the smuggling activities Crishi and Renée have been carrying out.

Jhabvala's skill in the use of an innocent narrator apparently unknowingly revealing sophistication and guile in others can be seen as Harriet continues to be unable to recognize what is before her eyes and what the reader has suspected all along. But because of Jhabvala's subtle presentation of Harriet's narration, the reader is never quite sure. In fact, the reader's path is in some ways close to that of Michael, idealism giving way to skepticism, and opposite to that of Harriet, her initial skepticism being replaced by obsession and finally disillusionment. Even when Crishi in a moment of intoxication reveals his genuine attitude toward the Rawul's meeting and by implication his whole Sixth World movement—"I don't care one fuck for your meeting. Not this much: not one fuck" (*TC*, 295)—Harriet continues to be duped by him. Nothing, it appears, not his frank admission of his desire for money, his clear revelation of his attitude toward the Rawul's movement, or the details of his criminal past, seems to be able to shake Harriet into an awareness of his true nature. Even when she knows Michael has been murdered, she goes along with Crishi's plans to present his death as suicide. The only explanation Harriet, as narrator, offers for this remarkable ability to close her eyes to the truth about Crishi is her desperate need for sex from him. This simply isn't enough to justify or even explain her infatuation, and it raises the questions, Where is Harriet now? How did she finally get away from Crishi? It also raises questions about the author's construction of a narrator who refuses to explain her present relation to the events she records in the narrative. This factor does not appear to be artistically justified or satisfying.

Michael, on the other hand, though he is, as Anna Sultan describes him and his sister, "self-centered, self-conscious, uptight, and definitely weird" (TC, 137), and though he too is taken in by Crishi and the movement, does have the sense to see that what he believed in is false. And Michael, unlike Harriet, does believe in the movement until late in the novel. He has the strength to admit that his commitment to the movement was misguided, and it is because he is prepared to admit his mistake, which means he is prepared to change his mind about donating his inheritance, that he is killed.

When Harriet does finally reach the Rawul's palace in Dhoka (in the closing scenes of the book), its appearance presents a stark contrast to her own home, Propinquity: "It was not very old—late Victorian perhaps, built around the same time as Propinquity—and was a mixture of Indian temple and English 'bungalow,' with arched verandas running all the way around it and a dome on top. It was huge—truly a palace—and lay in a wasted garden. But if the garden appeared wasted—dried and dead—that was nothing compared to the palace itself. From a distance, that is, when we first came in through the gates, it looked imposing and intact, but as we drew nearer, I could see that it was entirely derelict" (TC, 377). Like the Rawul's movement itself, the palace is a whited sepulcher empty of any saving graces of propinquity and indicates that nothing about the Rawul and his entourage is to be credited. That the palace has been stripped of everything of value—"everywhere only gaps and wounds, where some salable object had been" (TC, 377)—suggests that if the twins' inheritance was to pass into the hands of Crishi, the same fate would befall their homes.

This description of the pillaged palace leads to the question of the Rawul's sincerity. Has he too been duped by Crishi and Renée, or is he aware of what is going on? Early in the novel, for example, the Rawul is seen to be comfortable in the role of colonizer of Propinquity when he invites Harriet to help herself to breakfast "as if it were his house already"

(*TC*, 29). Yet the Bari Rani, when she tells Harriet about Renée's marriage to Rupert, adds a few words about the Rawul: "poor Rupert. I don't think he knows in the least what's going on. No one really knows—not the Rawul, he's much too up there in the clouds—only she knows, she and Crishi" (*TC*, 172). But the Bari Rani, as the Rawul's wife, is not a reliable person to voice his innocence. Moreover, the fact that she can speak so knowledgeably about Renée and Crishi suggests that she too knows what is going on. But it does appear that much of what goes on is kept from the Rawul, particularly the less seemly aspects of the funding of the movement: "there was the understanding that the Rawul was not to participate in these aspects of the work: that as the founder and figurehead of the movement he was not to know what had to be done to keep him afloat" (*TC*, 249). And the Rawul is frequently presented as sincere in his aims and in his belief in his movement: "Although so stout and sleek and middle-aged, the Rawul did give an impression of youth and idealism. And what he said was true—he and Michael were the same: They were the only two among us who still cared for the world movement, for Transcendental Internationalism, with a passion that the rest of us had dissipated on other, more personal ends of our own" (*TC*, 303).

Yet even if Harriet believes him to be sincere (and Harriet is nothing if not unreliable as a narrator), the Rawul certainly appears to accept without any qualms what he does know goes on. Thus, for example, he is willing to turn a blind eye to his followers beating up the local boys who were having a party in the grounds of Propinquity, even though their invasion (unlike that of the Rawul's followers) is benign, and later he leaves the room when Crishi assaults an Indian art dealer. By not speaking out against the violence, he is condoning it. Later Renée confirms the Rawul's complicity: "He knows very well what's going on" (*TC*, 349), and Renée's view of the Rawul's involvement must carry more weight than either Harriet's or the Bari Rani's. And as Henry Summerfield explains, "[f]or the assiduous reader of Ruth Jhabvala, one incident in Delhi will come near to damning him" ("Summerfield," 84). In a passage that echoes a scene from *A New Dominion* Father Tom tries to persuade Harriet to return home, just as Miss Charlotte in the earlier novel tries to persuade Margaret to leave Swamiji's ashram and go to the hospital. The Rawul appears to agree with Father Tom and tells Harriet, "Father thinks you should go home for a while. Go back to your family" (*TC*, 311). But like Swamiji, the Rawul deliberately supports Father Tom only halfheartedly, letting Harriet know that he wants her to stay.

If we are right to view the Rawul in a similar light as Swamiji in *A New*

Dominion, then he is indeed an unholy guru. The elderly, dying Babaji, the ex-leader of an earlier world movement, tends to be presented in a more favorable light than the Rawul and his followers, yet he too is damned when Harriet reports that "He loved nothing better than to tell me about all the girls who had come flocking to him; leaving behind their parents, friends, lovers, husbands" (*TC*, 203). For Jhabvala to present the Rawul in such a way that he can be seen as of the same ilk as Swamiji and Babaji can only confirm that he too is a knowing deceiver. We should not forget that in the West the Rawul's movement is supported by smugglers—of drugs as well as stolen art—and that in India his movement is promoted through corruption—through paid supporters bused in to boost his political ambitions, for example. In this regard it is instructive to note that, as Feroza Jussawalla explains, *dhoka* means *to dupe*.[8] The fact that he calls himself a Rawul when he is no longer justified in using the title immediately suggests his willingness to deceive people. Similarly, his empty palace and ruined heritage suggest that his movement is equally empty and is a dupe. Yet while the Rawul may be duping people who join his movement, it appears that he in turn is being duped by Crishi and Renée (who, we presume, were responsible for selling whatever treasures his palace once held). It is a case not simply of the West being conned by the unscrupulous, deceitful East but of naive inheritors being duped by deceitful disinheritors.

The irony that has been such a trademark of Jhabvala's writing and is a founding principle of this novel is nowhere more evident than when, as part of his Founder's Day celebrations, the Rawul has himself weighed against a pile of books, against "the Wisdom of all ages and all cultures" (*TC* 278). The books he is weighed against "included the Bible, the Koran, Plato, the Dhammapada, the Questions of King Milinda, the Tibetan Book of the Dead, the Tao Teh Ching, Carlos Casteneda, St. Augustine, Plotinus, Kierkegaard—it was at Kierkegaard that the Rawul started to swing up so that a few volumes had to be taken off to get him even and then put on again, with some fine adjustment to get it right" (*TC*, 279). The suggestion is clearly that the wisdom of the Rawul's movement is equal to the combined wisdom contained in all the weighty (and not-so-weighty) tomes that are piled on the other side of the scales. Alternatively, the Rawul can be seen as an overweight old man, ludicrously sharing a huge pair of scales with a pile of secondhand books.

The twins, Michael and Harriet, are easy targets for the dubious exploiters who organize the movement, and they share much in common with the seekers of Jhabvala's later Indian novels. And while Crishi may well be a deceitful Indian who preys on the "innocent" twins, as various religious scoundrels prey on the Western seekers of earlier novels and stories, it must be remembered that Jhabvala is not only critical of the Indian dupers—she also condemns the characters from what Rekha Jha describes as "the weak-willed West" who allow themselves to fall foul of such hoaxes.[9] When he first brings the Rawul and his entourage to Propinquity, Michael describes the movement as "*Om*, the real thing" (*TC*, 17), which, Harriet tells the reader, was what she and Michael had been searching for as they grew up. And much later Harriet relates the story told to her by Paul (the follower who is beaten up by Crishi at Propinquity and later spends time in a Turkish jail) as he lies suffering from a fever in a Delhi hotel room. Harriet tells us that Paul had envied Michael when they first met because Michael "came and went where he pleased and did what he pleased; he wasn't bound by anyone. Paul himself had been that way once upon a time—it was why he had come here in the first place: to get away, from home, from his family, from himself, his own personality as it has been formed by these outward circumstances; not to be bound by anything" (*TC*, 353). This is the goal of the many seekers in Jhabvala's fiction who have in one way or another been crippled by middle-class European or American upbringings, but it is rarely what they find. Paul, like other seekers before him, found not fulfillment but disillusionment and another form of bondage:

But by the time he had met Michael, he had been more bound by circumstances than he would have ever thought possible. They all were, all the group around Crishi. Some of them, like Paul himself, had been in jail and, expelled as undesirable, were waiting for new travel documents; these documents were being got for them by Crishi, and it was he who was paying their bills in the hotel and doling out money to them. It wasn't only that they were materially dependent on him—most of them couldn't live any longer without him telling them what to do and arranging everything for them; and with some of them it was even worse—they needed him emotionally—like the German girl Ursula, who had been pregnant by someone or other, and when she couldn't get into Crishi's room, she had slept on the stairs outside it. (*TC*, 353)

Jhabvala sets up a series of circumstances in order to investigate the interrelationships between cultural and personal life. The involvement of the twins with the movement is inevitable, because of what their culture, their parents, and their own personalities have made them and because of the process therein, and the personalities involved are what interests Ruth Jhabvala. This aspect is most clearly expressed in the third and final section, "In the Rawul's Kingdom," which is set wholly in India. As I argued in chapter 4, images of a hostile Indian landscape, the references to the heat and the dust, become visual representations of the physical and mental discomforts of people who find themselves in distressing situations or relationships; such images do not necessarily suggest an authorial attack on India or Indians. Not surprisingly, then, the Indian landscape is consistently presented as hot and dusty in *Three Continents*. The view from the hotel room in Delhi is typical of many descriptions of the Indian landscape in Jhabvala's fiction: "Everything appeared dry, white, parched by the sun like skeletons" (*TC*, 284). And when Michael is found to be missing and Harriet desperately searches for him, the descriptions of the heat and dust of Delhi are used to show how distressing their situation in India is for the twins: "It was hot, the season had changed, we had got into the Delhi summer, and its heat and dust blew through the open rickshaw in which I sat" (*TC*, 351). Noticeably, there are none of the positive descriptions of the sky to balance the heat and dust in this novel as there are in novels like *A Backward Place*, because there are no Western characters like Judy who are comfortable in India. Consequently, Harriet, Sonya, and to an extent Michael spend much of their time in their hotel with the curtains closed to shut out the hostile Indian environment. Even in Dhoka Harriet immediately draws the curtains to shut out the landscape she has traveled through for two days on the train.

England, though, where the twins also reside with the movement, is presented equally negatively—as cold, wet, and gray. Harriet and everyone else lived in "one of those gloomy old five-story English houses with high ceilings and tall narrow windows" (*TC*, 157). The house overlooked a garden, "but all the time we were there," Harriet laments, "it was never warm enough to sit out; anyway, it was usually raining. I spent a lot of time looking out of the window at the trees in the rain" (*TC*, 157). In contrast to the negative description of both the Indian and the English landscapes, America is frequently presented positively in relation to the twins, just as Paul is able to think positively of Yorkshire, where he would be far better off than he is in Delhi or anywhere else where Crishi has a hold on him.

In *Three Continents* the pattern of the East-West encounter in one of Jhabvala's early novels, *Esmond in India*, has been fully reversed. In *Esmond in India* it is Esmond who is portrayed as the evil force, who colonized Gulab and corrupts Shakuntala. It is Indians like these two women and to an extent their families too who are presented as the victims of the English exploiter. This portrayal of the East-West encounter began to change in later novels. In *A Backward Place* the West is no longer the successful exploiter of the East, as Etta's unsuccessful attempts to persuade Guppy to take her to Europe show. But the East is not yet cast in the role of exploiter: although Etta thinks that Bal is exploiting Judy, most readers would not see her as a victim. In Jhabvala's next novel, *A New Dominion*, however, the unprincipled Swamiji is all too successful in his exploitation of the naive, impressionable European women who come within his clutches. And by *Three Continents* the reversal of the colonization pattern is complete. In this book Indians travel to America and Europe to exploit the naive Westerners. Esmond has been replaced by the even more unscrupulous Crishi, the evil force who colonizes Harriet far more ruthlessly than Esmond ever did his hapless victims.

But if Indians are now the dupers, the evil exploiters of Jhabvala's novels, we must remember that they have learned their lesson from the Englishmen like Esmond who were the deceivers of Jhabvala's early fiction. Jhabvala's critical portraits of Indians may reflect her own position on the Indian wheel of fortune she is still strapped to, yet they are also in part portrayed as the inevitable result of a colonial past with which, as she demonstrated in *Heat and Dust*, Jhabvala has little sympathy. It is concerns like this that make Jhabvala an important postcolonial novelist.

Chapter Seven
Ruth Prawer Jhabvala and the Critics
Conclusion

The following passage appears in Upamanyu Chatterjee's novel *English, August: An Indian Story*:

> Menon picked up his papers from the table. "Have you read this?" He handed Agastya a large green book, Ruth Prawer Jhabvala's *Heat and Dust*. "I borrowed it from the Collectorate Library because I was told it was about an Assistant Collector's life in the British days. But it's not really about that." Agastya flipped the pages. Many passages were underlined; all of them seemed to be about an Assistant Collector touring in the early morning to avoid the title. Comments in red ballpoint in the margin: "Not necessary these days to wear sola topee. Relic of the Raj. The bureaucracy to be Indianized," and "Difficult question. An officer's wife *should* mix with others, but without jeopardizing the dignity of office."
> "Someone's been scribbling in the book," said Agastya.
> "Yes, I thought I should put down what I feel strongly about so that other readers have at least a choice of opinion. Otherwise they might think that even now this is all that goes on in an Indian district."[1]

This passage is significant for a number of reasons. First, it suggests that the author, Upamanyu Chatterjee, assumes that many of his readers will be familiar with Jhabvala's novel. Second, Menon assumes that other borrowers will select Jhabvala's book from the shelves of the collectorate library. Third, there is an implicit assumption that those readers will interpret the novel in a particular way, which Menon feels obliged to challenge. And here Chatterjee aligns Menon with those Indian critics who feel that *Heat and Dust* provides a wholly negative portrait of India, based on cultural misunderstanding. But perhaps more than anything, the passage gives *Heat and Dust* a mantle that might previously have been worn by *A Passage to India*. The passage I have quoted would read equally well if "E. M. Forster's *A Passage to India*" was substituted for "Ruth Prawer Jhabvala's *Heat and Dust*." This regressive intertextuality (the reference to *Heat and Dust*, which in turn calls *A Passage to India* to mind) actually suggests the strength of Jhabvala's novel and the important place it has earned in the fiction of India.

Moreover, the passage deliberately captures the tone of resentment that many critics, particularly Indian ones, have displayed toward *Heat and Dust*. Nissim Ezekiel, for instance, puts forward the view that Jhabvala's hatred of India is reflected in this novel, making "her fiction a monstrous distorting mirror."[2] In a later piece he pulls no punches when he states, "I found *Heat and Dust* worthless as literature, contrived in its narrative structure, obtrusive in its authorial point of view, weak in style, stereotyped in its characters and viciously prejudiced in its vision of the Indian scene."[3] In the same article he asks of the title *Heat and Dust*, "Is there not a demeaning motive in this characterising of a country and its culture in terms of climate and the least valuable, so to speak, element lying on the physical territory designated?" (Ezekiel, 6). The answer must be no—there is no demeaning motive in Jhabvala's title or in her use of the heat-and-dust metaphor in her novels, and she is by no means suggesting that heat and dust represent the sum total of India and its culture. If there is in any way a demeaning motive in Jhabvala's title, then it is in the same way that there is a demeaning motive in Dickens's descriptions of a cold and foggy London. Dickens's descriptions apply metaphorically not to the city itself but to the corrupt institutions—the legal system, the circumlocution office, and so on—that are coldhearted, impersonal, and foggy insofar as they obscure the truth. But this is by no means criticism by Dickens of London in toto or of all Londoners.

Because *Heat and Dust* treats the British raj, it inevitably invites comparison with earlier raj novels. Jhabvala is aware of this factor (not only in her use of *A Passage to India*) and in *Heat and Dust* she sets about destroying some of the myths of raj fiction. The title *Heat and Dust*, rather than demeaning India as Nissim Ezekiel believes, conjures up, at least for the Western reader, romantic images of that country. Heat is the climate of love and passion, and it is not uncommon for the hero of an exotic romance film to ride out of the flat desert landscape, covered in dust (though not quite enough to hide his good looks), to rescue or claim the beautiful heroine. For Ezekiel to suggest that the English public would be upset by any work of fiction set in England that bore a title like "Cold and Fog" is to seriously misunderstand the literary context and metaphoric implications of the title. "Cold and Fog" is a *literal* translation that depends on a misunderstanding of both Jhabvala's title *Heat and Dust* and the British conception of India as the passionate, exotic "other" and on a failure to consider the tradition of the British adventure story. Moreover, *dust* also conjures up images of the past, of history, of that which is finished but, ironically, of course, is not finished—as is the case with the narrator's relationship with Olivia and the 1923 story.

India may well be seen as a living hell for the European derelicts outside A's Hotel early in *Heat and Dust*, but it is also presented as a paradise on earth later in the same novel (*HAD*, 180). In an article entitled "The Blinds Drawn and the Air Conditioner On" Eunice de Souza presents another very one-sided argument when she criticizes Jhabvala's portrait of Gulab in *Esmond in India* while ignoring the acid pen directed at the Englishman Esmond Stillwood.[4] This seems a good example of the sort of cultural focus that has characterized much (though, of course, not all) of the negative criticism aimed at Jhabvala. And if there are faults with Jhabvala's early portraits of India and Indians, surely *To Whom She Will* is an astonishing picture for anyone to paint after only two years in India. Why, too, should Jhabvala be attacked because some of her *characters* (Esmond or Etta, for example) come to hate India? this is the worst sort of confusion between author and character.

In contrast to the negative assessments of Ezekiel and de Souza, another Indian critic, N. S. Pradhan (who takes Ezekiel to task in his article), sees no fault in Jhabvala's presentation of India or Indian characters and dismisses such criticism as "literary chauvinism."[5] In his early full-length study of Jhabvala Vasant Shahane sets out a clear appreciation of Jhabvala's position when he writes:

> In my view Jhabvala should not be linked with other creative Indian writers in English such as Mulk Raj Anand, Raja Rao or R. K. Narayan, nor with women novelists such as Kamala Markandaya or Nayantara Sahgal. She is in a way unique and the advantages as well as disadvantages of her literary situation are particular to her. The advantage lies in her special position of being a European living in India; the disadvantage, too, lies in her not being a genuine, grassrooted Indian. She can therefore be detached, ironic and satirical. She can view the game of human affairs in an Indian family from a point of view which is both objective and unsentimental.[6]

There is, then, a clear division of opinion about Jhabvala's work among Indian critics. In Britain and America there has been no such marked range of response. In both countries the critical attention paid to

Jhabvala's work has been generally favorable. Although some Indian critics, like Ramlal Agarwal, Meena Belliappa, and, more recently, Rekha Jha, write favorably about Jhabvala's fiction, there remains an apparent East-West division in the critical assessment of her work. Salman Rushdie believes this dichotomy is due at least in part to the very nature of the beast "Commonwealth Literature." In "'Commonwealth Literature' Does Not Exist," an essay written in 1984, Rushdie writes:

> I said that the concept of "Commonwealth literature" did disservice to some writers, leading to false readings of their work; in India, I think this is true of the work of Ruth Prawer Jhabvala. . . . You see, looked at from the point of view that literature must be nationally connected and even committed, it becomes simply impossible to understand the cast of mind and vision of a rootless intellect like Jhabvala's. In Europe, of course, there are enough instances of uprooted, wandering writers and even peoples to make Ruth Jhabvala's work readily comprehensible; but by the rules of the Commonwealth ghetto, she is beyond the pale. As a result, her reputation in India is much lower than it is in the West.[7]

Perhaps for similar reasons too there is a small number of critics who have written extensively on Jhabvala. Notable among these are Haydn Williams and Yasmine Gooneratne.

This seems an appropriate place to consider the question of what makes a novel Indian. Is it the author's birth or the setting and subject matter of the novel?—because the fact that Jhabvala is perceived as an outsider, a foreigner writing about India seems to lie at the heart of the negative critical reception to her writing. It seems to me that Jhabvala's early novels are most definitely Indian, though by *A Backward Place* she does begin to move away from purely Indian domestic and social concerns and to focus instead on European characters in an Indian setting. But this does not mean that those novels are not Indian novels. Jhabvala's more recent works of fiction have been set largely in the United States and are most certainly not Indian novels, yet they share the universal concerns of much of her Indian fiction. The picture becomes clearer, perhaps, if the situation of a writer like Buchi Emecheta is considered. She is a Nigerian writer, and *The Joys of Motherhood*, for example, is demonstrably a Nigerian novel. But other Emecheta novels are set in London. The author is the same African woman, but these latter books are not African novels. Jhabvala is not an Indian writer, but she does write Indian novels and stories. It is salient too that in the name she chooses to write under—Ruth Prawer Jhabvala—she deliberately maintains her German maiden name, rather than disguising her outsider identity by writing under the name of Ruth Jhabvala or R. P. Jhabvala.

The range and diversity of Jhabvala's literary output, which includes novels, short stories, screenplays, and personal essays, and the high standard she has achieved in all the various genres she tackles are remarkable.

The themes of the East-West encounter and the expatriate experience are always present in Jhabvala's writing, and her own rootless position, her own unusual triple heritage, is mined to provide an objectivity that is uncommon if not unique in its insight. As a foreigner living in India Jhabvala was (and is) in an ideal position to write about these concerns with great assurance. An awareness of history and politics, though frequently overlooked, is also present in Jhabvala's fiction, manifesting itself in the presence of characters who had been involved in the struggle for freedom or who suffered during Partition, as well as in the obvious presence of the British raj in *Heat and Dust*.

The essays "Myself in India" and "Moonlight, Jasmine and Ricketts," and the lecture-cum-essay "Disinheritance" provide unusual insights and show that Jhabvala is indeed a skilled practitioner of the personal essay. In particular, "Myself in India" is an honest and brave attempt to explain her feelings for the country in which she still lived at the time of the essay's writing. This essay, while being universally welcomed in the West, has often attracted harsh criticism from within India. Yet as the title clearly emphasizes, it is not about India, but about Ruth Prawer Jhabvala in India. The India of the essay is Jhabvala's personal India, and as such it is only one India, one writer's very personal view of that vital country, which, along with her other essays, provides essential insights for the critic interested in her fiction. There are, after all, many Indias.

To an extraordinary degree Jhabvala's reputation has rested on her novel *Heat and Dust*. This is no doubt at least partly due to its being awarded the Booker Prize and to its secondary success as a film—which event brought both the novel and its author to the attention of many readers not familiar with her earlier fiction. (Indeed, since the screenplay of the Merchant-Ivory-Jhabvala film version of E. M. Forster's *A Room with a View*, for which Jhabvala won an Academy Award, many filmgoers know of her as an accomplished scriptwriter, without knowing her fiction.) I don't think, however, that *Heat and Dust*, though a very fine novel, is Jhabvala's best work: *A Backward Place* and *In Search of Love and*

Beauty are both more skillful, subtle, rich, evocative, sophisticated, effortless, and moving achievements.

With the benefit of hindsight it may well be that no single work of Jhabvala's will stand out from her oeuvre. And here the comparison with Jane Austen is useful once more. Like Austen (or like Dickens), Jhabvala is likely to be remembered for the body of her writing rather than for any single work. She is a writer whose work will stand the test of time.

Notes and References

Chapter One

1. Patricia W. Mooney, "Another Dimension of Living," *Newsweek*, 31 October 1977, 52; hereafter cited in text.
2. Bernard D. Nossiter, "Enjoying the Fruits of Detachment," *Washington Post*, 9 December 1975, C2.
3. The general biographical information in this chapter is gathered from Ruth Prawer Jhabvala's Neil Gunn Memorial Lecture, "Disinheritance" (published in *Blackwood's Magazine*, July 1979, 4–14; hereafter cited in text) and from the articles listed in the "Interviews and Profiles" section of the Selected Bibliography (specific references cited in the notes that follow).
4. Bernard Weinraub, "The Artistry of Ruth Prawer Jhabvala," *New York Times Magazine*, 11 September 1983, 112; hereafter cited in text.
5. Unsigned, "A Heritage of Lonely Wandering," *Observer*, 10 April 1983, 7; hereafter cited in text.
6. Nirad C. Chaudhuri, *The Continent of Circe* (London: Chatto & Windus, 1965), 17.
7. Caroline Moorehead, "A Solitary Writer's Window on the Heat and Dust of India," *Times* [London], 20 November 1975, 16.
8. Unsigned, "A Novelist of India Reflects 2 Worlds," *New York Times*, 17 July 1973, 31; hereafter cited in text.
9. Ruth Prawer Jhabvala, "Introduction: Myself in India," in *How I Became a Holy Mother and Other Stories* (Harmondsworth, England: Penguin, 1981), 9; hereafter cited in text as "Myself in India." The stories in this collection were originally published by John Murray as *An Experience of India* (1971) and *How I Became a Holy Mother* (1976).
10. Ramlal Agarwal, "Outsider with Unusual Insight," *Times of India*, 25 March 1973, 11; hereafter cited in text.
11. Anna Rutherford and Kirsten Holst Peterson, "*Heat and Dust*: Ruth Prawer Jhabvala's Experience of India," *World Literature Written in English* 15, no. 2 (1976): 375; hereafter cited in text.
12. Ramlal Agarwal, "An Interview with Ruth Prawer Jhabvala," *Quest* no. 91 (1974): 36.

Chapter Two

1. H. Moore Williams, "English Writing in Free India (1947–1967)," *Twentieth Century Literature* 16, no. 1 (1970): 9.
2. In the Penguin edition Jhabvala has changed the name of Amrita's

grandfather from Pandit Ram Bahadur Saxena to Rai Bahadur Tara Chand. "Rai Bahadur" is an honorific title conferred on Hindus by the British raj (Khan Bahadur being the equivalent title for a Muslim). On the other hand, "Pandit" is a traditional title; to put the two titles "Pandit" and "Rai Bahadur" ("Ram" presumably should have been "Rai") together simply would not ring true. Why the name should be further changed from Saxena to Tara Chand is less obvious, except that the latter is more complete—Saxena being the equivalent of a family name only.

3. Ruth Prawer Jhabvala, *To Whom She Will* (1955; reprint, Harmondsworth, England: Penguin, 1985), 9; hereafter cited in text as *TWSW*.

4. Yasmine Gooneratne, *Silence, Exile, and Cunning: the Fiction of Ruth Prawer Jhabvala* (New Delhi: Orient Longman, 1983), 35; hereafter cited in text.

5. Linda Warley, "The Cuckoo's Nest: House and Home in Two Early Novels by Ruth Prawer Jhabvala," in *Passages to Ruth Prawer Jhabvala*, ed. Ralph J. Crane (New Delhi: Sterling Publishers, 1991), 21.

6. Ruth Prawer Jhabvala, *The Nature of Passion* (1956; reprint, Harmondsworth, England: Penguin, 1986), 176–77; hereafter cited in text as *NOP*.

7. Haydn Moore Williams, *The Fiction of Ruth Prawer Jhabvala* (Calcutta: Writers Workshop, 1973), 20; hereafter cited in text.

Chapter Three

1. Ruth Prawer Jhabvala, *Esmond in India* (1958; reprint, Harmondsworth, England: Penguin, 1980), 31; hereafter cited in text as *EII*.

2. Meena Belliappa, "A Study of Jhabvala's Fiction," *Writer's Workshop Miscellany*, February 1971, 26.

3. Laurie Sucher, *The Fiction of Ruth Prawer Jhabvala: The Politics of Passion* (London: Macmillan, 1989), 15; hereafter cited in text.

4. Ruth Prawer Jhabvala, *The Householder* (1960; reprint, Harmondsworth, England: Penguin, 1980), 40; hereafter cited in text as *TH*.

5. Ruth Prawer Jhabvala, *Get Ready for Battle* (1962; reprint, Harmondsworth, England: Penguin, 1981), 10; hereafter cited in text as *GRB*.

6. Ramlal Agarwal, *Ruth Prawer Jhabvala: A Study of Her Fiction* (New Delhi: Sterling Publishers, 1990), 49; hereafter cited in text.

7. It is strange that Ramlal Agarwal should conclude that Vishnu is "like Hari and Viddi, who initially want to do something novel but finally end up by preferring security and comforts of the joint family system" (*Ruth Prawer Jhabvala: A Study of Her Fiction*, 50); it seems clear to me that this is exactly what Vishnu has escaped.

Chapter Four

1. Ruth Prawer Jhabvala, *A Backward Place* (1965; reprint, Harmondsworth, England: Penguin, 1980), 93; hereafter cited in text as *BP*. When this novel was first published, Jhabvala had been living in India for 14 years.

2. Ruth Prawer Jhabvala, "A Spiritual Call," in *A Stronger Climate* (1968; reprint, London: Granada, 1983), 90; hereafter cited in text as *SC*.

3. In an interview with Yolanta May (*New Review*, 2, no. 21 [1975]: 53–57) Jhabvala suggests that this remark, because it is made by Clarissa, was meant ironically. She does, however, admit that there is some truth in it.

4. In her Neil Gunn Memorial Lecture Jhabvala says of *A Passage to India*, "I'd read *Kim* and *A Passage to India*, as literature; neither made me want to go to India nor became anything more than another literary landscape to be enjoyed" ("Disinheritance," 8).

5. Yasmine Gooneratne, "Irony in Ruth Prawer Jhabvala's *Heat and Dust*," *New Literature Review*, no. 4 (1978): 45.

6. Anna Rutherford and Kirsten Holst Peterson, "*Heat and Dust*: Ruth Prawer Jhabvala's Experience of India," *World Literature Written in English* 15 (1976): 377.

7. Ruth Prawer Jhabvala, *A New Dominion* (1972; reprint, London: Granada, 1983), 10; hereafter cited in text as *ND*.

8. A parallel to this parable occurs in *Heat and Dust* when Leelavati, the beggar woman, is left to die alone by the inhabitants of Satipur. It is only when she is discovered by the narrator, who calls Maji, that Leelavati is spared the "experience" of dying uncared for.

9. V. S. Pritchett, "Snares and Delusions," *New Yorker*, 16 June 1973, 106.

10. E. M. Forster, *A Passage to India* (1924; reprint, Harmondsworth, England: Penguin, 1979), 281; hereafter cited in text.

11. Haydn M. Williams, "Mad Seekers, Doomed Lovers, and Cemeteries in India: On R. P. Jhabvala's *Heat and Dust* and *A New Dominion*," *New Literature Review*, no. 15 (1988): 20.

12. Richard Cronin, "*The Hill of Devi* and *Heat and Dust*," *Essays in Criticism* 26, no. 2 (1986): 144; reprinted in Richard Cronin, *Imagining India* (London: Macmillan, 1989), 161–76. Cronin's remark is not entirely valid, as Harry, though without talent himself, is a tool of Jhabvala's talent. Nor am I convinced that Jhabvala believes Harry is a more trustworthy witness than Forster.

13. Santha Rama Rau, *A Passage to India* [a play from the novel by E. M. Forster] (London: Edward Arnold, 1960).

14. Ruth Prawer Jhabvala, *Heat and Dust* (1975; reprint, London: Futura, 1976), 103; hereafter cited in text as *HAD*.

15. See "Myself in India," 14. Of her own experience Jhabvala writes: "So I am back again alone in my room with the blinds drawn and the air-conditioner on."

16. Yasmine Gooneratne suggests that "the stories of Olivia and the narrator are brought together through Major Minnies' monograph 'on the influence of India on the European consciousness and character' (which applies

equally to them both) and run finally into one as the narrator pauses by Olivia's last home on a mountainside to complete her journal before continuing her climb towards the truth she seeks, and to which she believes Olivia's experience points the way" (*Silence, Exile and Cunning*, 219).

Chapter Five

1. Ruth Prawer Jhabvala, "An Experience of India," in *How I Became a Holy Mother* (Harmondsworth, England: Penguin, 1981); 120, hereafter cited in text as *HM*. The stories in this collection were originally published by John Murray as *An Experience of India* (London, 1971) and *How I Became a Holy Mother* (London, 1976).

2. Ruth Prawer Jhabvala, "Commensurate Happiness," *Encounter* 54, no. 1 (1980): 3–11; hereafter cited in text as "Happiness."

3. Ruth Prawer Jhabvala, "Grandmother," *New Yorker*, 17 November 1980, 54–62.

4. Paul Scott, *Staying On* (1977; reprint, London: Granada, 1978), 255.

5. Ruth Prawer Jhabvala, "The Englishwoman," in *How I Became a Holy Mother* (New York: Harper & Row, 1976), 24. This story is not included in British editions.

6. Ruth Prawer Jhabvala, "The Widow," in *Like Birds, like Fishes* (1963; reprint, London: Granada, 1984), 58; hereafter cited in text as *LBLF*.

Chapter Six

1. Laurie Sucher, for example, describes Jhabvala as "a writer who had built a career on the interpretation of India to the West" (*Politics of Passion*, 169).

2. Ruth Prawer Jhabvala, *In Search of Love and Beauty* (1983; reprint, Harmondsworth, England: Penguin, 1984), 5; hereafter cited in text as *SLB*. For a discussion of the Greco-Roman mythological allusions in *In Search of Love and Beauty* see Sucher, 177–84.

3. Jennifer Livett, "Propinquity and Distance: The America of Jhabvala and Bellow," in *Passages to Ruth Prawer Jhabvala*, ed. Crane, 64–78; hereafter cited in text.

4. See Henry Summerfield's essay "Holy Women and Unholy Men: Ruth Prawer Jhabvala Confronts the Non-rational," *Ariel* 17, no. 3 (1986): 85–101.

5. There are glimpses of Fanny Price, the young heroine of Jane Austen's *Mansfield Park*, in the character of Natasha—and the fact that Natasha catches a chill after getting soaked in the Hamptons is a very Austenish touch.

6. Ruth Prawer Jhabvala, *Three Continents* (1987; reprint, Harmondsworth, England: Penguin, 1988), 383; hereafter cited in text as *TC*. In the original John Murray (London, 1987) and William Morrow (New York, 1987) editions of the novel the Rawul's movement is called the "Fourth World

movement"; in later editions, including the Penguin one, the name is changed to the "Sixth World movement."

7. Henry Summerfield, "Religion Becomes Political: Ruth Prawer Jhabvala's Tenth Novel," in *Passages to Ruth Prawer Jhabvala*, ed. Crane, 81; hereafter cited in text.

8. Feroza Jussawalla, "On Three Continents: The 'Inside' is the 'Outside,'" in *Passages to Ruth Prawer Jhabvala*, ed. Crane, 87.

9. Rekha Jha, *The Novels of Kamala Markandaya and Ruth Jhabvala* (New Delhi: Prestige Books, 1990), 82.

Chapter Seven

1. Upamanyu Chatterjee, *English, August: An Indian Story* (London: Faber, 1988), 39.

2. Nissim Ezekiel, "A Distorting Mirror?" *Times of India*, 4 January 1976, 10.

3. Nissim Ezekiel, "Cross-Cultural Encounter in Literature," *Indian P.E.N.* 43 nos. 11 and 12 (1977): 5; hereafter cited in text.

4. Eunice de Souza, "The Blinds Drawn and the Air Conditioner On: The Novels of Ruth Prawer Jhabvala," *World Literature Written in English* 17, no. 1 (1978): 219–24.

5. N. S. Pradhan, "The Problem of Focus in Jhabvala's *Heat and Dust*," *Indian Literary Review* 1, no. 1 (1978): 16.

6. Vasant Shahane, *Ruth Prawer Jhabvala* (New Delhi: Arnold-Heinemann, 1976), 13.

7. Salman Rushdie, "'Commonwealth Literature' Does Not Exist," in *Imaginary Homelands* (London: Granta Books, 1991), 68.

Selected Bibliography

PRIMARY SOURCES

For each book I have listed the first English edition, the first American edition, and the paperback edition referenced in this study. Titles are listed chronologically.

Novels

To Whom She Will. London: Allen & Unwin, 1955; New York [published as *Amrita*]: Norton, 1956; Harmondsworth, England: Penguin, 1985.
The Nature of Passion. London: Allen & Unwin, 1956; New York: Norton, 1957; Harmondsworth, England: Penguin, 1986.
Esmond in India. London: Allen & Unwin, 1958; New York: Norton, 1958; Harmondsworth, England: Penguin, 1980.
The Householder. London: John Murray, 1960; New York: Norton, 1960; Harmondsworth, England: Penguin, 1980.
Get Ready for Battle. London: John Murray, 1962; New York: Norton, 1963; Harmondsworth, England: Penguin, 1981.
A Backward Place. London: John Murray, 1965; New York: Norton, 1965; Harmondsworth, England: Penguin, 1980.
A New Dominion. London: John Murray, 1972; New York [published as *Travelers*]: Harper & Row, 1973; London: Granada, 1983.
Heat and Dust. London: John Murray, 1975; New York: Harper & Row, 1976; London: Futura, 1976.
In Search of Love and Beauty. London: John Murray, 1983; New York: Morrow, 1983; Harmondsworth, England: Penguin, 1984.
Three Continents. London: John Murray, 1987; New York: Morrow, 1987; Harmondsworth, England: Penguin, 1988.

Short Story Collections

Like Birds, like Fishes. London: John Murray, 1963; New York: Norton, 1964; London: Granada, 1984.
A Stronger Climate. London: John Murray, 1968; New York: Norton, 1968; London: Granada, 1983.
An Experience of India. London: John Murray, 1971; New York: Norton, 1972.

How I Became a Holy Mother. London: John Murray, 1976; New York: Harper & Row, 1976; Harmondsworth, England: Penguin, 1981. The U.S. editions of this collection of stories include an additional story, "The English-woman." The Penguin edition includes the stories previously published by John Murray as *An Experience of India* and *How I Became a Holy Mother.*

Out of India. London: John Murray, 1987; New York: Morrow, 1987; Harmondsworth, England: Penguin, 1989. The stories in this volume are selected by Ruth Prawer Jhabvala from her previous four collections.

Uncollected Short Stories

"Before the Wedding." *New Yorker*, 28 December 1957, 28–32.

"Better than Dead." *New Yorker*, 24 May 1958, 30–36.

"The Elected." *New Yorker*, 30 April 1960, 40–45.

"Wedding Preparations." *Kenyon Review* 23 (1961): 408–22.

"Of Love and Sorrow." *Writers Workshop Miscellany*, no. 10 (1962): 31–35.

"Light and Reason." *New Statesman*, 19 July 1963, 73–74.

"Foreign Wives." *London Magazine*, January 1968, 12–22.

"A Very Special Fate." *New Yorker*, 29 March 1976, 27–35.

"Parasites." *New Yorker*, 13 March 1978, 34–43; *London Magazine*, August/September 1980, 3–20.

"A Summer by the Sea." *New Yorker*, 7 August 1978, 26–34; *London Magazine*, July 1979, 14–30.

"Commensurate Happiness." *Encounter* 54, no. 1 (1980): 3–11.

"Grandmother." *New Yorker*, 17 November 1980, 54–62.

"Expiation." *New Yorker*, 11 October 1982, 44–51.

"Farid and Farida." *New Yorker*, 15 October 1984, 40–50.

Miscellaneous

"Moonlight, Jasmine, and Ricketts." *New York Times*, 22 April 1975, sec. 1, 35.
    Important piece in which Jhabvala writes about her attitudes toward India.

"Disinheritance." *Blackwood's Magazine*, July 1979, 4–14.
    Indispensable. The text of Ruth Prawer Jhabvala's Neil Gunn Memorial Lecture, in which she speaks about her background of disinheritance and its effect on her writing.

SECONDARY SOURCES

In this list I have included useful interviews, important books, and major articles.

Interviews and Profiles

Agarwal, Ramlal. "An Interview with Ruth Prawer Jhabvala." *Quest*, no. 91 (1974): 33–36.
    Jhabvala provides answers to questions about her attitudes toward India, her writing, and literary influences.

May, Yolanta. "Ruth Prawer Jhabvala in Conversation with Yolanta May." *New Review* 2, no. 21 (1975): 53–57.
    A conversation about Jhabvala's later Indian novels, her background, and her attitude toward India.

Mooney, Patricia W. "Another Dimension of Living." *Newsweek*, 31 October 1977, 52.
    Concentrates on Jhabvala's attitude toward India and her move to the United States.

Moorehead, Caroline. "A Solitary Writer's Window on the Heat and Dust of India." *Times* [London], 20 November 1975, 16.
    A particularly illuminating profile that discusses Jhabvala's changing attitudes toward India, her film-writing career, *Heat and Dust*, and her plans to move to New York.

Nossiter, Bernard D. "Enjoying the Fruits of Detachment." *Washington Post*, 9 December 1975, C2.
    Jhabvala talks about her Jewish background, the characteristics she feels Jews share with Hindus, her recent Booker Prize, and her plans to move to New York.

Rutherford, Anna, and Kirsten Holst Petersen. "Heat and Dust: Ruth Prawer Jhabvala's Experience of India." *World Literature Written in English* 15 (1976): 373–77.
    A formal interview prefaced by a brief discussion of Jhabvala's work. Questions are asked about the influence of film on her fiction.

Weinraub, Bernard. "The Artistry of Ruth Prawer Jhabvala." *New York Times Magazine*, 11 September 1983, 64–5, 106, 110, 112, 114.
    An indispensable interview/profile. Jhabvala speaks frankly about her early life and her career as a writer.

Unsigned. "A Novelist of India Reflects 2 Worlds." *New York Times*, 17 July 1973, 31.
    Jhabvala speaks about her early reactions to India and how those reactions have changed over the years.

Unsigned. "A Heritage of Lonely Wandering." *Observer*, 10 April 1983, 7.
    A judicious overview of Jhabvala's life.

Critical Studies

Agarwal, Ramlal. "Outsider with Unusual Insight." *Times of India*, 25 March 1973, 11.

Looks at some of the reasons why Jhabvala has been neglected by Indian critics.

————. *The Fiction of Ruth Prawer Jhabvala.* New Delhi: Sterling Publishers, 1990.

A disappointing survey that discusses the novels on the basis of plot summaries. Earlier pieces are included in the appendixes.

Asnani, Shyam K. "Jhabvala's Novels—A Thematic Study." *Journal of Indian Writing in English* 2, no. 1 (1975): 38–47. A useful introductory essay that deals with the novels to *A Backward Place.*

Belliappa, Meena, "A Study of Ruth Prawer Jhabvala's Fiction." *Banasthali Patrika*, no. 12 (1969): 70–82. Reprinted in *Writers Workshop Miscellany*, no. 43 (1971): 24–40.

Dealing with the novels to *A Backward Place*, the first part of the essay looks at contrast as a source of social comedy; the second considers the fiction as social documentation.

Blackwell, Fritz. "Perception of the Guru in the Fiction of Ruth Prawer Jhabvala." *Journal of Indian Writing in English* 5, no. 2 (1978): 6–13. Contrasts the swami in *The Householder* with the guru figures in later Indian novels.

Crane, Ralph J. "Ruth Prawer Jhabvala: A Checklist of Primary and Secondary Sources." *Journal of Commonwealth Literature* 20, no. 1 (1985): 171–203. An annotated bibliography, comprehensive to the end of 1981.

————. "Ruth Prawer Jhabvala's Sky: Escape from the Heat and Dust?" In *Inventing Countries: Essays in Post-Colonial Literatures* (*Span*, no. 24), Edited by William McGaw, 178–89. Wollongong, Australia: SPACLALS, 1987. Discussion of Jhabvala's treatment of the sky and landscape in *A Backward Place*, *A New Dominion*, and *Heat and Dust.*

————, ed. *Passages to Ruth Prawer Jhabvala.* New Delhi: Sterling Publishers, 1991.

Contains the following essays, all previously unpublished: Haydn M. Williams, "A Retrospective Look at Ruth Prawer Jhabvala's Career as a Novelist: The Indian Novels"; Linda Warley, "The Cuckoo's Nest: House and Home in Two Early Novels by Ruth Prawer Jhabvala"; Joanne Tompkins, "Universal Satire or Eurocentrism? The Marginalization of the Animal in Ruth Prawer Jhabvala's *Esmond in India*"; Paul Sharrad, "Passing Moments: Irony, Ambivalence and Time in *A Backward Place*"; Ralph J. Crane, "A Forsterian Connection: Ruth Prawer Jhabvala and *A Passage to India*"; Jennifer Livett, "Propinquity and Distance: The American Novels of Jhabvala and Bellow"; Henry Summerfield, "Religion Becomes Political: Ruth Prawer Jhabvala's Tenth Novel"; Feroza Jussawalla, "On Three Continents: The 'Inside' is the 'Outside'"; Ron Shepherd, "'Yes, something is wrong': Obscure Irritant in Ruth Prawer Jhabvala's Short Stories"; and Yasmine Gooneratne, "Ruth Jhabvala's Screen Plays."

Cronin, Richard. "*The Hill of Devi* and *Heat and Dust.*" *Essays in Criticism* 26, no. 2 (1986): 142–59. Reprinted in *Imagining India*, 161–76. London: Macmillan, 1989.

Excellent essay. Shows how Jhabvala draws on Forster's book for her knowledge of British India.

———. "Riding the Beast: Ruth Prawer Jhabvala in India." In *Imagining India*, 34–44. London: Macmillan, 1989.

Good, wide-ranging piece that considers the rich source of Jhabvala's talent—her tussle with India.

de Souza, Eunice. "Four Expatriate Writers." *Journal of the School of Languages* 4, no. 2 (1976–77): 54–60.

Compares Jhabvala and Jean Rhys. Acknowledges *The Householder* and *Like Birds, like Fishes* as sensitive and perceptive but sees neither of these qualities in the later works.

———. "The Blinds Drawn and the Air Conditioner On: The Novels of Ruth Prawer Jhabvala." *World Literature Written in English* 17, no. 1 (1978): 219–24.

A highly critical essay that shows how Jhabvala has upset the sensibilities of certain Indian critics.

Ezekiel, Nissim. "Cross-Cultural Encounter in Literature." *Indian P.E.N.* 43, nos. 11 and 12 (1977): 4–8.

Interesting for its strongly worded attack on *Heat and Dust.*

Gooneratne, Yasmine. "Irony in Ruth Prawer Jhabvala's *Heat and Dust.*" *New Literature Review*, no. 4 (1978): 41–50.

A detailed analysis of the narrator.

———. *Silence, Exile and Cunning: The Fiction of Ruth Prawer Jhabvala.* New Delhi: Orient Longman, 1983; 2d ed. 1990.

An excellent study of Jhabvala's fiction and her writing for the cinema. Builds on work published in a number of earlier articles.

———. "Literary Influences on the Writing of Ruth Prawer Jhabvala." In *Language and Literature in Multicultural Contexts*, Edited by Satendra Nanden, 141–68. Suva, Fiji: University of the South Pacific and ACLALS, 1983.

An illuminating article that focuses on eighteenth-century influences.

———. "Apollo, Krishna, Superman: The Image of India in Ruth Prawer Jhabvala's Ninth Novel." *Ariel* 15, no. 2 (1984): 109–17.

Shows how in *In Search of Love and Beauty* Jhabvala brings together her own triple heritage.

Jha, Rekha. *The Novels of Kamala Markandaya and Ruth Jhabvala.* New Delhi: Prestige Books, 1990.

Solid thematic approach that looks at the novels of Markandaya and Jhabvala in tandem. Concentrates on the novels to *Heat and Dust*.

Mukherjee, Meenakshi. "Inside the Outsider." In *Awakened Conscience*, edited by C. D. Narasimhaiah, 86–91. New Delhi: Sterling Publishers, 1978.
Includes some perceptive comments about Jhabvala's position as an "outsider."

Pradhan, N. S. "The Problem of Focus in Jhabvala's *Heat and Dust*." *Indian Literary Review*, 1, no. 1 (1978): 15–20.
Interesting for its dismissal of the hostile Indian critical response to Jhabvala's writing.

Sastry, L. S. R. Krishna. "The Alien Consciousness in Jhabvala's Short Stories." In *The Two-Fold Voice* (Essays on Indian Writing in English), Edited by D. V. K. Raghavacharyulu, 164–73. Viyayawada-Guntur, India: Navodaya Publishers, 1971.
Helpful discussion of the stories in Jhabvala's first two collections. Focuses primarily on the East-West encounter.

Shahane, Vasant A. *Ruth Prawer Jhabvala*. New Delhi: Arnold-Heinemann, 1976.
A useful introductory study of the fiction to *Heat and Dust*. A number of chapters have been reprinted in periodicals and collections of essays.

Sucher, Laurie. *The Fiction of Ruth Prawer Jhabvala: The Politics of Passion*. London: Macmillan, 1989.
Valuable contribution to Jhabvala studies. Close reading, from a feminist perspective, of the latest four novels and a number of related stories. Concentrates on the quest for love and beauty.

Summerfield, Henry. "Holy Women and Unholy Men: Ruth Prawer Jhabvala Confronts the Non-rational." *Ariel* 17, no. 3 (1986): 85–101.
Illuminating essay on the swami figures in Jhabvala's fiction.

Williams, Haydn Moore. "The Yogi and the Babbitt: Themes and Characters of the New India in the Novels of R. Prawer Jhabvala." *Twentieth Century Literature* 15, no. 2 (1969): 81–90.
At one end of the spectrum Lalaji (*The Nature of Passion*) and Gulzari Lal (*Get Ready for Battle*) are seen as Babbitts, while at the other end the swami in *The Householder* and Sarla Devi (*Get Ready for Battle*) are seen as Yogis.

———. *The Fiction of Ruth Prawer Jhabvala*. Calcutta: Writers Workshop, 1973.
This early book is a valuable introduction to the first six novels.

Index

The Author

Ralph Crane is a lecturer in the English department at the University of Waikato, Hamilton, New Zealand. Born in Preston, England, in 1957, he has degrees from the University College of Swansea, Wales; the University of Victoria, Canada; and the University of Tasmania, Australia. He has edited a collection of essays entitled *Passages to Ruth Prawer Jhabvala* and is the author of *Inventing India: A History of India in English-Language Fiction*.